THE CHIEF

THE
CHIEF

Carl Madison's
Life in Football

CLINT CROCKETT
FOREWORD BY SCOTTI MADISON

The Chief: Carl Madison's Life in Football

© 2022 by Clint Crockett

Editors: Earl Tillinghast, Rayna Batiste, Deborah Froese
Cover and Interior Design: Emma Elzinga

Indigo River Publishing
3 West Garden Street, Ste. 718
Pensacola, FL 32502
www.indigoriverpublishing.com

Ordering Information:
Quantity sales: Special discounts are available on quantity purchases by corporations, associations, and others. For details, contact the publisher at the address above.

Orders by US trade bookstores and wholesalers: Please contact the publisher at the address above.

Library of Congress Control Number: 2022911341
ISBN: 978-1-954676-34-3 (paperback)   978-1-954676-35-0 (ebook)

First Edition

With Indigo River Publishing, you can always expect great books, strong voices, and meaningful messages. Most importantly, you'll always find . . . words worth reading.

CONTENTS

FOREWORD

THOSE OF US fortunate enough to play a sport in high school or college will all agree that somewhere along the way, a coach had an impact on us. For a few, it could have been a bad experience playing for someone who stole the luster from their dreams. But the coaches the rest of us so fondly remember are the ones who challenged us to reach a higher level, to reach beyond our natural physical ability. They encouraged us to dedicate ourselves to a team cause outside of our own personal ambition.

Those coaches were usually tough, maybe even closer to downright mean, and exerted their will to shape us, mold us, and drive us to become overachievers—not only on the field of glory but taking that same desire to win into the field of life. They taught the exceptional qualities of sacrifice, hard work, respect, determination, and commitment that are critical to winning in the game of football, yet far more valuable beyond.

My uncle, "the Chief" Carl Madison, was that man for me and for hundreds of other benefactors over his half-century career. He grew up poor, and poverty closed many doors for him. Carl realized his only way out of Atmore, Alabama was through playing sports. He and his brother Charles were exceptional athletes early on, and by the ninth grade of their high school years, they had regular roles on the varsity football team.

Coach Madison also excelled in basketball and baseball in high school. If there was a season with a ball in it, the two brothers always tried their hand at it and were determined to conquer that sport.

Who could possibly write a story about this poor Native American boy born in Uriah, Alabama and later became one of the winningest high school football coaches in the state of Florida? It would take someone who personally played for him, but even more critically, it would need to be someone with a passion for the game who recognizes the Chief's quality of dedication. Such a writer is Clint Crockett.

Clint grew up in Pensacola, Florida. At an early age, his father, James, nurtured his love for football. James is a lifelong fan who attended Ole Miss during the glory years of the program. He saw his school post a 36–3–3 record with three unbeaten regular seasons and Southeastern Conference championships during his four years there. As a child, before his father began taking him to Ole Miss games in the late 1970s, Clint listened to "The Ballad of Archie Who" over and over on his record player—a song about quarterback Archie Manning. During his first year of attending games, he witnessed the Rebels defeat Notre Dame at Mississippi Veterans Memorial Stadium in a season that would see the Fighting Irish go on to win the national championship. Without a doubt, Clint became hooked on football.

A move back to Pensacola, Florida from Oxford came just in time to experience the rise of Coach Carl Madison's fame. It was somewhere during his freshman year at Tate High School that Coach Madison challenged Clint to play at Tate. For those who never played under him, Coach's practices were probably mythical, and the stories of stick fighting and hanging off the back of the stadium would bounce from locker to locker in the hallways. Yet those who dared to enter into a Carl Madison's practice garnered satisfaction walking away from the "death camp," especially after a loss. Clint, like the rest of us, survived and not only lived to tell about it, but he aspired to write about his coach and not be satisfied with just telling stories.

Clint was one of us, a chosen one, someone privileged to have played for "the Chief." Thus, he felt the growing pains found in perfection through memorable practices like everyone else. In addition, his dedication to research as he wrote *The Chief: Carl Madison's Life in Football* is second to none, and Clint's work allows former players the opportunity to reminisce about factual history. Clint's delivery in the book is something each reader can treasure when traveling back in time to those glory days. I found it humbling to relive some of those close losses and quite exhilarating to read about a comeback victory. These events happened forty years ago, yet it seems like it just happened yesterday.

Coach Madison was tough on everyone but especially tough on those closest to him. He made it clear to everyone that he did not play favorites, so he went to the opposite extreme to demonstrate that was the case. In addition to me, both his sons, Mark and Sky, played for him. So did his cousin, Paul Madison. On the gridiron, we all received our fair share of verbal reprimands—some deserving—and a few extra choice words beyond what the other players got.

I know firsthand because I was there as his quarterback as well as his nephew. I stood in line with my cousins—as did every other football player—to receive correction when we were told over and over to "run it again."

Carl Madison is certainly quite memorable as my uncle and I love him dearly, yet he was legendary as my head football coach. He was bigger than life for everyone that he coached, and although small in frame and weight, no one was more intimidating to the high school kid. You did what he asked—even if it meant running through a brick wall. Clint helps you understand why this was the case in his book.

I know this book will bring back memories. Clint Crockett far exceeded my expectations with *The Chief: Carl Madison's Life in Football*. I was almost ready to change back into my shoulder pads, helmet, and uniform. If only they would fit.

SCOTTI MADISON
Tate High Class of 1976

PREFACE

FROM A YOUNG age, I was exposed to my father's voracious reading habit, and I later majored in English in college. Both of those experiences contributed greatly to my own love of books. After eventually reaching the point in my life where I knew I had to write, Carl Madison was the obvious choice as my subject.

Carl is a legendary figure in high school football who influenced many young men during his life. Some of those young men recognized the impact he had while they played for him. For many others, myself included, months and years passed before they truly gained an appreciation for the lessons he taught them and how their lives were impacted by the time they spent under his tutelage. In my case, it took the challenges of being a husband, a father, and having a career.

Interpreted through my firsthand experience with Coach Madison at Tate and interviews with others who know him, this book covers everything from his playing days at Atmore High School, Texas Tech, and Troy State to his coaching stops at Ernest Ward, Milton, Forest Park, Tate, Ernest Ward (again), Pine Forest, Westover, Pensacola High, Milton (again) and finally, Jackson Academy.

I was living in Tampa, Florida in June of 2005 when I called Coach Madison to inform him of my intention to write a book about him. We had not spoken in almost seventeen years. During our conversation, he told me that he would be coaching in the Fourth Annual Native All-

Star Game in Lawrence, Kansas on July 1. Madison had coached in the inaugural affair and, with his nephew Scotti assisting him, won against Herman Boone of "Remember the Titans" fame.

Madison and Boone both had tremendous records as high school football coaches but were also chosen due to their Native American roots. Boone's mother was Cherokee, Madison's Poarch Creek.

I immediately made plans to attend. I drove thirteen hundred miles to Lawrence, stopping in Birmingham and Memphis along the way, before arriving at the campus of Haskell Indian Nations University, the matchup location. Madison invited me into the locker room before the game, so I went straight there. Upon entering, the first voice I heard was Madison's as he addressed his team. Not wanting to disturb his pregame speech, I stood in the corner.

Madison spotted me and smiled. With tongue firmly planted in cheek, he introduced me to his players. "He's going to write a book about me. If he talks to any of you, by God, you better say something good about me."

Though his clearly outmanned West squad lost to the East, it was a great day and evening. I enjoyed dinner with Coach Madison and his family members who had also made the trip and spent time speaking with his wife Grace, his brother Charlie, and two of his children, Becky and Sky. Over the next few years, there were many other meetings and conversations with Madison, and much of what he related is included in the following pages. I also spoke with several of his former players and coaches. I learned something new about the man in every one of those conversations.

This book was years in the making. I conducted interviews with approximately thirty people. They included former teammates, assistant coaches who served under Madison, opposing coaches, his players, family, and friends. Most of the interviews occurred in person. I also met with Carl Madison numerous times, even staying at his house during one of my visits. All of the interviews were recorded.

Before newspapers were digitized and readily available online, countless hours were spent in libraries going through old newspapers. I probably should have paid tuition at the University of West Florida where I toiled the hours away going through microfilm of the *Pensacola News* and *Pensacola News Journal.* In addition to my initial drive to Kansas, trips to Alabama, Georgia, and the Florida panhandle were taken to conduct interviews and for library research. I later moved to Madison, Mississippi and made multiple trips back to the Florida panhandle from there as well, putting thousands of miles on multiple vehicles, listening to hundreds of songs, and devouring dozens of audio books during my travels working on the project. I enjoyed every minute of it.

Life intervened in various ways in the years from 2005–2020. I had periods of diligent work on the book and others where it was put aside. Other writing projects occurred simultaneously, and I became discouraged about this one, unsure of my ability to do it justice. I am not sure the book would have ever been completed had it not been for a phone call from Erik Hector in the fall of 2020.

Erik was two years older than me at Tate, an outstanding defensive player on the 1980 state championship team and someone I'd seen once in the past thirty-eight years or so. Erik told me about an event being planned to celebrate Carl Madison's ninetieth birthday and to name the field at Tate High School in his honor. He asked me to participate in the planning. That led me to dive back into the manuscript and commit to finishing it. Over the next few months, Erik provided incredible encouragement to me.

During the initial preparation for this book, it occurred to me that over the course of my life I've had conversations with hundreds, perhaps thousands, of people, but there is only one person I encountered whose very first words to me I could recall: Carl Madison.

In early 1981, as a freshman at Tate High School in Gonzalez, Florida, I was walking through the boys' locker room when Carl Madison saw me.

He stopped and asked, "Why aren't you playing football?"

This question has likely been asked of hundreds of boys at various high schools over the years, however, I imagine in most cases it was presented to very large young men who looked like they belonged on a football field. I was five foot eight inches, weighed about 135 pounds at the time, and had no idea why he would ask me such a question. I didn't imagine he even knew me at all. At the time, he was the coach of the 4A Florida state football champions—the highest classification then—and I was a freshman nobody. It's possible he knew of my making the baseball team or playing for one of the local little league football teams that past fall. I wasn't sure.

"I plan to play football at Tate next year," I answered.

"Then you'd better get into the football player's P.E. class," he told me.

Within a couple of days, I did.

So began my own introduction to the world of legendary high school football coach Carl Madison. I only spent two and a half years under him since he was let go from Tate in a highly controversial move just before my senior year. Many years later, disagreements remain about what actually transpired, and they are addressed in the book. Although I experienced a brief time under Coach Madison, he influenced many of my values and ideals.

My introduction to Madison's complex nature occurred during my junior year. During one of our practices, my good friend Gordon Whatley knocked me unconscious, sending me to the hospital with a severe concussion. During the evening hours, I received a visit from Carl Madison, of all people, who had come to check on me. I could not have been more surprised.

Weeks later when finally able to return to practice, I dropped a short shuffle pass.[1] Coach Madison immediately ordered the play rerun and directed the offensive lineman not to block anyone.

I was hit hard and dropped the ball again.

"Run it again," he said.

---

1   A "shuffle pass" is basically a short forward pitch from the quarterback to a wide receiver running across the middle behind the line of scrimmage.

This happened at least three more times—all without the benefit of any blockers. I was destroyed by multiple defensive linemen every time. It makes me laugh to think about it now, but it wasn't funny at the time. That was just Coach Madison, and it would have been foolish on my part to expect anything different. If a lesson was intended, it was probably "I hope you enjoyed your time off, but don't expect me to change my coaching style just because you were out with an injury. You're well enough to be out here now. Welcome back to reality."

Another incident further demonstrated his complex nature to me. During my senior year, after his dismissal from Tate, Madison served as an assistant coach at Pensacola High School. Early in the season, I received a phone call from him one evening. He told me that he had been following me in the papers and wanted to offer his congratulations on the success I was having. I don't recall my response because it caught me by such surprise. I am sure I thanked him.

It was a very nice gesture on his part, but the wheels began spinning in my head. We played Pensacola High School (PHS) in a few weeks. Was he trying to psych me out? I doubted it, but you never could tell with Carl Madison. When we finally played PHS later in the season, we entered unbeaten. They beat us 33–26, and the thing I remember most is lining up close to the PHS sideline with time running out. It was apparent we were going to lose. I looked over and saw Coach Madison, crouched over, hands on his knees. We made eye contact, and he winked at me. Who knows what he was thinking? When I reminded him of this many years later, he did not recall it happening. I never forgot, and it still causes me to shake my head.

Ironically, having a different coach for my senior year ended up being a good thing for me personally. I had a good season, making the Northwest Florida All-Area team—along with a promising young Escambia freshman named Emmitt Smith. Yet I cannot help but wonder how our team would have fared with Madison as coach.

We were a senior-laden squad and finished 8–2. The final loss came in the last game of the season to our district rivals and then number two rated team in the country, the Woodham Titans by a 21–13 score. I would have gladly traded any individual success to win that game. Almost forty years later, the loss still bothers me, though time has added perspective.

Carl Madison's career in football was not without controversy, and he had his share of detractors. Some good people disagreed with his methods and made it known. He was dismissed from coaching positions on two occasions, and those are addressed within these pages. The reader can come to their own conclusion whether either instance was justified.

For most of his career, he was certainly "old school" in the tradition of Bear Bryant—and that just wasn't for everyone. No doubt some very talented athletes over the years chose not to play football because they just did not want to subject themselves to Carl Madison four to five hours daily. However, he believed his approach was the proper one to prepare his young men—not just for football but for life. The great majority of those who played for him swear by him to this day, and many applied the lessons they learned as 14- to 18-year-old boys throughout their lives. Madison coached young men who went on to play football professionally, but he also coached future business leaders, doctors, attorneys, military servicemen—including a major general, coaches, educational leaders, and good, solid working and family men. His impact on people's lives reached well beyond the years they played for him.

Madison recognized the value of good leadership early in his playing days, and that contributed greatly to his approach as a football coach. He viewed part of his responsibility as creating future leaders, on and off the football field. John Ryan Colvin, now a physician, quarterbacked Madison's final two state championship teams at Jackson Academy in Alabama.

Years later, Colvin still remembers what he learned from Madison during that time. "People in leadership positions need to be the first one there. The last to leave. They need to be setting examples for everyone in terms of work ethic. It's so important that the people that you work with, or play with or people that you're around, family or friends, [that] they . . . see that you are passionate and motivated and focused on what you're doing. That is contagious. We saw that in him [Madison]. That's how he became as successful as he was."

Almost all his players feared and respected him during their playing days. Some even considered him a father figure, though certainly not the touchy-feely kind. He came from a generation of men who rarely showed any kind of sensitivity. I certainly did not experience that side of him in my playing days other than the hospital visit. I've since learned about many examples of his compassion and caring for young men who needed guidance and a positive direction in their lives. He provided that. His own upbringing undoubtedly influenced his approach to coaching young men.

Carl Madison is referred to as "the Chief" by many, though it is difficult to pin down exactly how he came to be known that way. Some speculate that his Tate defensive coordinator, Bobby Taylor, was the one who originally gave him the moniker. Taylor is on record calling him by that nickname in an interview with the *Pensacola News Journal* during the Tate days. Whether or not it had anything to do with his Poarch Creek Indian background is uncertain, but that would make sense. Madison never took offense to the nickname. In fact, he embraced it.

The book is not intended to be a complete biography of the man. One thousand pages would not suffice to tell that story. To be clear, though I mention many of the controversies in his career, my representation of Carl Madison from the interviews and articles is shaped by my own perspective. I admire the man but understand there are those out there who do not share that feeling and may recall some of the stories recounted here differently or have their own stories. I intend to tell the story of his life in football and his influence. I learned an incredible amount about him during my research and through the numerous interviews I conducted, laughing plenty and shaking my head countless times. I found myself rooting for his old teams—even at schools other than Tate.

Perhaps most importantly of all, I gained a much greater appreciation for the man Carl Madison and what he accomplished beyond the football field. There's a reverence for him among his former players and so many went on to do amazing things in their lives. Most of them would say that Coach Madison was a huge influence, and they are where they are today due in part to what he taught them. Hopefully, this book captures a small part of that.

A complete list of source materials is included in the bibliography at the end of the book. Manuscript comments and dialogue are drawn from original newspaper articles or interviews I conducted and in some instances have been edited for clarity and brevity.

CLINT CROCKETT

August 2021

CHAPTER ONE
HARDSCRABBLE BEGINNINGS

THERE ARE PLENTY of stories throughout history and even today about people who came from hardscrabble beginnings and went on to the highest levels of success in their professions. But they are the exception, not the rule. It is an arduous process to grow out of poverty into that kind of success, and it requires special character and determination. Carl Madison had those characteristics and more. He faced significant obstacles from his early life all the way through his playing and coaching days. Few would have blamed him had he chosen a different path and lived an average life. But that wasn't in his makeup. He was determined to rise above his circumstances and, to paraphrase William Faulkner, not just endure but prevail.

In 1931, the Great Depression was still in its infancy in America. Though unemployment rates were high, they would not see their peak until a couple of years later. On January 16 of that year, William Carl Madison was born in Uriah, Alabama, delivered at home to Thomas and Vivian Madison by a local doctor. Vivian came from the local Poarch Band of Creek Indians, making Carl half Native American.

At the time of his birth, one of the more popular movie serials shown in theaters around the country featured Red Grange, the famed "Galloping Ghost" football star of the National Football League's Chicago Bears. Though never as widely celebrated as Grange, Carl Madison would one day leave a legacy in football too. He would even be referred to as his own "Galloping Ghost" by a sportswriter in his high school playing days. But no one could have anticipated all that in Uriah, Alabama in January of 1931.

A year and a half later, another son arrived to the Madisons. They named him Charlie. The family spent the first eight years of Carl's life in Uriah before moving twenty miles south to Atmore, Alabama.

Carl's early childhood was not unlike that of many others of his day, or later days, in rural America. He spent much of his time climbing trees, swinging from ropes, and playing pickup football or baseball games with the other local boys. Skinned knees and elbows, cuts and bruises were daily occurrences for him due to his activities. Nearly every Christmas, he and Charlie would receive some sort of new ball to play with. They were also given a .22 rifle one year and while shooting at targets in a field, a bullet missed its target, traveled well beyond it and the field, eventually striking a gentleman in the leg. When this was discovered, they prepared for what they thought would be the beating of their lives from their father by stuffing shingles in their pants to protect them from the blows. As a result, when their father came home and told them to sit down, they could not do so without their legs sticking straight out. Fortunately for Carl and Charlie, neither the beating nor any legal issues resulted from the careless event, and things resolved peacefully.

Like most other boys, Carl had heroes. The heroes of his youth were Harry Gilmer, the Alabama quarterback known for the jump pass who led his team to a Rose Bowl victory over the University of Southern California (USC) in 1946; Bobby Layne, the famed Texas quarterback who went on to play fifteen seasons in the National Football League (NFL); Layne's high school and later NFL teammate, Heisman trophy winner Doak Walker of Southern Methodist University (SMU); and another Heisman winner and later pro football star, Paul Hornung. He tried to emulate them when he played pickup football and later for his school.

Atmore, Alabama was founded in the 1860s and originally called

Williams Station. It was renamed Atmore in 1897 to honor C.P. At-more, the General Ticket Agent on the Louisville Nashville Railroad that passed through the town on its way to Mobile. During the time Carl Madison grew up, the town had a population of less than five thousand and was an agricultural center. Agriculture and timber are still primary economic factors in its economy today, though it is generally considered a manufacturing town. In the mid-1900s, people came into town for livestock sales on Saturdays, and many of the local men worked in Mobile at the shipyards. But what made Atmore in Madison's days was the high school football team. They were treated like royalty with a free movie at the local theater and free meal at one of the restaurants on game day.

Floyd Adams, who was inducted into the Alabama Baseball Coaches Association Hall of Fame in 2012, grew up in Atmore also and was a few years younger than Madison. He later worked with Madison at both Milton and Tate High Schools as the offensive line coach. Adams experienced great success as the head baseball coach at Tate and later at Jefferson Davis Junior College in Alabama.

Of those days in Atmore, Adams said, "Every Friday night the stores were closed, and everybody went to the football game. Atmore was a very progressive little town; one of the better small towns in the South." Of Madison, he said, "He was one of the older boys everybody looked up to. One I tried to be a lot like."

At the Atmore—officially known as Escambia County High School—Herbert Barnes was the football coach for all but Madison's senior year. Barnes was an agriculture teacher at the school, but in 1943 during World War II, the head football coach was called into service in the Pacific theater with four games remaining in the season, and Barnes became the coach. Barnes, originally from north Alabama, attended Furman University on a football scholarship and later graduated from Auburn with a degree in Agriculture. Those who played for him at Atmore have always referred to themselves as "Barnes Boys" and they called him "Mr. Barnes," never "Coach Barnes."

To this day, Carl Madison still refers to him as Mr. Barnes. "Man, he was a mean guy," Madison said later. "Cuss . . . he could really cuss."

On one occasion, the local Baptist preacher decided to attend one of Barnes' Atmore practices. He did not stay long and never returned to the practice field. Barnes took competition seriously and discouraged his boys from helping opponents off the ground after the whistle. Carl Madison took note of this and practiced the same philosophy when he embarked upon his coaching career. As with Barnes, few if any preachers spent time at Madison's practices during his many years of coaching.

Atmore ran the single wing with an unbalanced line under Barnes, meaning more lineman lined up on one side of the center rather than having the typical two to three on either side. In the single wing, the ball was snapped directly to one of the running backs. The quarterback rarely handled the ball and was primarily a blocker. The offense was designed to confuse the defense, and Barnes worked his Atmore team until they could run it almost to perfection. Madison was hugely influenced by Barnes as anyone who ever played for him could attest.

World War II was just coming to its conclusion when Carl Madison began high school. Victory over Japan Day—or V-J Day—was on September 2, 1945, and he started his freshman-year classes that same month. He began practicing with the varsity football team and was anxious to see how he would fare against older and bigger boys.

The *Atmore Advance* article prior to the season called the Atmore team "light and young." Many of the older boys in town had left high school to join the service and were stationed overseas. Only thirteen lettermen returned. A list of "other aspirants" included Carl and his younger brother Charlie.

One could get a season ticket for the Atmore Fighting Blue Devils for $3.50 in 1945. Although opening the season with four straight victories, Madison did nothing to distinguish himself.

But that all changed against Evergreen.

The October 25 edition of the *Advance* read "Atmore's fighting Blue Devils buried Evergreen's Aggies under a 41–0 score here last Friday night, and Coach Herbert Barnes introduced a new grid star to local football fans. Playing his first game of high school football [he had actually seen some brief action earlier], Carl Madison, a 128-pound halfback who is in the ninth grade, threw bullet passes, was in on every tackle, and outran everything on the field."

Carl had never received attention like that in his life. The article gave him the incentive he needed to become a great ballplayer. "People bragged on me. I said, 'Man. This is great.' I really started trying to develop myself where I'd be better. I'd work and run thinking I would be better."

Madison would later claim on many occasions in his coaching career that it wasn't about him, and that the attention should be on the players. While he likely felt that to some degree, here was an early public admission that he did, in fact, enjoy attention. He would get plenty of it in his life because of football.

Against Flomaton, Madison completed five of eleven passes for eighty-six yards—which he would later say "wasn't too good"—in a 27–0 victory. Despite Madison's own thoughts, passing was yet to be a prominent part of any high school offense, and five of eleven was considered respectable. It caused the *Advance* to refer to him as "Bombsight Madison." Although he had moments of greatness during that season, he was not one of the major players due to his age. Atmore went on to finish the season undefeated for the first time since 1925.

After his ninth-grade year, Madison's parents separated. His mother moved to Fairhope and his father to Mobile. Carl and Charlie went with to live with their mother, but before he began tenth grade, a group of people from Atmore contacted Vivian to ask if the boys would come back to Atmore if someone provided their room and board. Frank Curry, a local businessman, led the group. He had played football at Auburn and was a prominent supporter of the Atmore program. When asked by their mother what they would like to do, the boys agreed they would prefer to return to Atmore. It was home. They had friends and wanted to continue playing ball there.

Carl and Charlie lived with the Welch family during Carl's sophomore and junior years. The Welches had twin boys, Wallace and Walter,
who were a year ahead of Carl in school and on the football team. Wallace played quarterback while Walter was a lineman. Walter remembered
Carl being an outstanding football player from a very young age and said
as far back as fifth grade that "he threw better than anybody else."

This wasn't the first time that the Welches took boys into their
home. They did so on previous occasions to help others facing difficult
situations. The two years the Madison boys lived with the Welches, they
had jobs and shared a room. They studied there, ate all meals there, and
were treated just like members of the family. In fact, Thomas Madison
told Mr. Welch that "if the boys needed whacking, then whack them."
But Carl and Charlie caused little trouble during their time there and
the whacking proved unnecessary.

The years living in Atmore without his parents were tough for Carl,
but he was driven to succeed in sports. He later spoke about feeling as
though people were constantly talking about his brother Charlie and
him. That they didn't have a mother and father around and would never
amount to anything. That drove Carl to succeed. He wanted to prove
to the community that they were wrong. He would become somebody
special.

Before his sophomore season, six former GIs returned from the war
to play football for the Blue Devils. Madison later spoke about their return. "They were men. You'd see them in the shower with tattoos all over
their bodies and that would scare you." The team had a drill where they
ran one hundred yards with a tackler every ten yards. "These guys would
rough you up."

Once again, the opener came against Tate, a team "heavy and stud-
ded with many veterans." An ad in the *Atmore Advance* for Joyner's Ice
Cream Hqd, invited everyone to "Meet Your Friends Here After the
Game of Any Time for a Refreshing Ice Cream Treat." The ice cream
was enjoyable that night following a 19–7 win over the Aggies.

Atmore won its next four contests before taking on Fairhope. With one tie, the undefeated Pirates had not lost at home since 1943. In front of the largest crowd ever to see a Fairhope game, Madison scored the first touchdown in a 14–0 victory. The October 31 edition of the *Atmore Advance* read, "The Atmore Blue Devils boarded the Fairhope Pirates ship and hauled down the Jolly Roger that had waved unscarred since 1943."

A perfect season to that point came crashing down for Carl with three games remaining. He and his brother Charlie were ruled ineligible to play due to issues with their residency. Because neither their mother nor father lived in the district, they could not suit up. Coach Barnes broke the news to an understandably disappointed team. The boys didn't feel they had done anything wrong, because although it was true that their parents weren't living in the district, *they* were. Not being able to play was a difficult pill to swallow, and it isn't completely evident Carl learned a lesson from it since he had battles during his coaching career over player residency requirements—not all of which he won.

With Carl and Charlie watching from the sidelines, Atmore tied Brewton T.R. Miller 7–7 before winning its final two contests. Madison was named a second-team all-county back by the *Advance* and the November 21 edition stated, "The Madison brothers will be eligible again next year [unless some little technical, unjustifiable rule is found]."

They regained their eligibility in 1947. When Carl entered his junior year, he once again found himself vying for a position with another former GI. This time it was Judson Brawner, recently returned from a tour with the Marines. Brawner was a strong player and had been a key member of the unbeaten 1945 Atmore squad.

Carl, on the other hand, was not a power runner, but he was hard to tackle. Walter Welch only remembered one person, Booker Stewart, from Bay Minette, ever getting a good hit on him. "I started to go over and congratulate him because none of us ever had. He would twist at the last second so you couldn't hit him cleanly."

Later, as a coach, Madison would utilize many more running backs than the majority of his competitors. It wasn't unusual for eight to ten different players to carry the ball in a game. Although he loved having a power back or two—the kind who could run over a defender—Madison couldn't help but have a fondness for the smaller, quicker, elusive types who played in the same style he once had.

The expectations were not high for Atmore going into the season after losing several players from the previous year. After a 41–0 win over Tate in the opener, it appeared the Blue Devils would be alright. Madison scored three times that night and "the highlight of the game came during the final period when Carl Madison broke loose for an eighty-six-yard touchdown dash with the entire Tate team trying to catch him."

Three straight victories followed before the Blue Devils faced an unbeaten- and unscored-upon Foley High. According to *The Atmore Advance*, in the first quarter Foley "sent a kick punt to Carl Madison. The Galloping Ghost scooped the ball up on his twenty and raced fifty yards to the Foley thirty." In a contest played in ankle-deep mud, the Atmore Blue Devils whipped Foley 34–0. Then came a defeat of another previously unbeaten squad, Brewton T.R. Miller in front of the largest crowd in the school's history—four thousand attendees.

Atmore closed the season with three more victories. They finished without a loss once again and stretched their overall unbeaten string to twenty-eight games. During the streak, they outscored their opponents 869–110. Madison considers the 1947 squad the best Atmore team he played on. The ice cream shop gave the local players a free milkshake whenever they scored a touchdown, and that season he scored over twenty.

"Boy, I had the milkshakes lined up then," he would later say.

The season proved to him that low expectations had no bearing on results. He would go on to coach many seasons with teams who had lost key players from the previous year. Because he took the time in practice to develop the younger boys and got them into games whenever an opportunity presented itself, most were typically prepared to ease into a bigger role. So, while outsiders might occasionally have low expectations for his teams, he rarely did—although he might go to great lengths to convince you otherwise.

Carl Madison was not valedictorian of his Atmore High class. Indeed, he did not aspire to great achievements in the classroom. In his own words, "I did what was necessary, enough to get by." But he did make every effort to get his work done early so he could do the things he enjoyed such as fish, hunt, and play sports.

Prior to Carl's senior football season, Coach Herbert Barnes resigned to return to teaching full time. The new coach, E.H. Penney, came from Monroeville where he'd experienced success. According to Madison, Penney "wasn't the disciplinarian Coach Barnes was. He was a good coach, but just wasn't as tough."

Madison's father remarried and returned to Atmore before Carl's senior year, so he and Charlie moved back in with him. It provided at least a sense of normalcy for the Madison boys, something they hadn't experienced in quite a while.

Expectations were high heading into the season. The opener came against Robertsdale, and Madison started his senior year start by running for two touchdowns and throwing another to Charlie in a 28–0 victory. Three more Atmore wins followed to run the unbeaten streak to thirty-two games.

Foley came next. The prior two seasons, Atmore had knocked them from the ranks of the unbeaten, but things would be much different this time around. Charlie was injured and did not play. Carl obviously missed him. Trailing 7–0 in the second quarter, Atmore drove to the Foley goal line where Madison threw an interception. They only threatened to score once more, and the final score was 7–0, ending their unbeaten streak.

"There's just a game you're gonna lose no matter what you do. I had games like that when I was coaching," Madison later said.

This perspective allowed Madison to move on quickly. Whether he won or lost a game, once it was over, his focus was on preparing to win the next one.

Atmore started a new streak by shutting out Brewton T.R. Miller 20–0 and followed that up with a win over Monroeville before finishing their season by tying Bay Minette 7–7. His high school football playing days were over. In them he experienced only one loss and two ties.

Despite being primarily a football player, during his senior year basketball season he learned a lesson that would help him later in life. During the season, Madison told his coach he planned to miss a game because he was dating an older girl at Montevallo College, and she had a dance that weekend that he wanted to attend.

His coach put his hand on Madison's shoulder and said, "Well Carl, turn your uniform in and y'all have a good time."

Madison did not attend the dance, and he employed that same coaching philosophy his entire career: that no player is more important than the team. "The only rule I ever really had is that if you miss practice without me knowing about it, you can't play," Madison said.

After demonstrating his significant talent during high school, Madison had options on where he would attend college. He visited Alabama. Auburn and Tulane also wanted him to come and see their campuses. His former Atmore teammate, Judson Brawner, graduated a year prior and ended up at Texas Tech, so Carl decided he would check things out there as well.

His visit to Lubbock impressed him. "I had been to New Orleans, Mobile, Montgomery, Pensacola. Went out there, and it was just really nice. They fed you steak and gravy every meal. I didn't really have a home. It was ideal."

Madison had never seen white gravy before, and he loved it. He may be the only football player in history to base his college choice partly on gravy, but that appeared to seal the deal. He chose Texas Tech.

As with most west Texas towns, Lubbock is not known for its scenery, though the locals and many who attended Texas Tech University love the place. In 1852, Army Captain Randolph Marcy was assigned to make a search of the region and make a recommendation regarding potential settlements. His official report described the area as "a region as vast and tractless as the ocean. It is a land where no man, savage or civilized, permanently abides. It spreads forth in a treeless, desolate waste of uninhabited solitude, which always has been, and must continue, to be uninhabited FOREVER."

But it eventually *was* inhabited, and by the time Madison made the almost thousand-mile journey from Atmore, the population was approaching one hundred thousand residents.

Madison headed to Lubbock in the summer of 1949 to play football for the Red Raiders and their coach, Dell Morgan. He had a solid first year, starting at quarterback on the freshman team, but with the outbreak of the Korean War, members of the National Guard received the call to active duty. Carl only joined the Guard so he could look after his brother Charlie, who had signed on. In a strange twist of fate though, Charlie did not receive the call to active duty and went on to the University of Georgia to play football.

Just prior to his military service, Carl Madison married Rachel Bricken. They eventually had three children together—Becky, Mark, and Sky—before later divorcing. Carl spent two years stateside in the Army at Fort Custer, Michigan and Fort Stewart, Georgia. While serving, he attended radio school and telephone lineman school.

By the time he returned to Texas Tech for his sophomore season, the entire coaching staff had changed. When he showed up for practice, they didn't know who he was, but when he told them he was Carl Madison, they said they had been waiting for him. Madison was thrilled to discover that Bobby Layne, one of his childhood heroes, was now the running backs' coach.

The September 6 edition of the *Lubbock Morning Avalanche* mentioned Madison as one of two new additions sparking the Red Raider offense in practices. "Little Carl Madison, who played freshman ball for Tech in 1950, returned to the Raiders Thursday after serving with an Alabama National Guard unit. The crafty quarterback lost no time in demonstrating he can still pass with the best."

Heading into the opener against West Texas State, Madison was listed among three quarterbacks taking snaps with the offense in practice. But his first action came in a B-team (Junior Varsity) game against

McMurry. In that contest he threw for 167 yards and ran for another thirty-three while the Red Raiders won 55–0.

The *Lubbock Morning Avalanche* stated, "Carl Madison made a serious bid for regular consideration as the starting quarterback next year . . . Carl showed one thing Friday night, he's the best passer on the Tech squad at present."

As things turned out, Madison did not have to wait until next year to see action on the varsity squad. The Red Raiders opened the season by beating West Texas State but proceeded to lose their next four games. With the University of Houston up next, he finally got his shot.

It was not a particularly successful debut. He threw four interceptions in a 20–7 loss to the Cougars. Still, his head coach, DeWitt Weaver, made a point afterwards to state that he thought Madison looked good running the offense. In his own coaching career, while Madison regularly criticized players for mistakes made during practices in front of teammates and other coaches, he rarely said anything negative regarding a player's performance to the press, regularly placing the blame on himself. Weaver set a good example for him in this regard.

In the week leading into a matchup with North Texas State, DeWitt announced several changes for his starting offense, among them that Carl Madison would be the quarterback. Joe Kelly of the *Lubbock Morning Avalanche* called the new backfield that included Madison "potentially great."

Madison started the game, but Weaver continued his practice of rotating quarterbacks throughout, and the Red Raiders fell short. He continued to rotate with others in the final four games of the season, while the Red Raiders won two and lost two.

During spring practice, Madison broke his collarbone and was unable to participate during a critical practice period for the season ahead. That summer Rachel obtained a job in Atmore that paid three hundred dollars a month, good money in 1952. Madison's father-in-law owned the Chrysler-Plymouth dealership there and Carl, thinking life was too short, decided not to return to college. He could stay in Atmore, work some, and hunt and fish.

Madison stayed out of school for a year and a half, but during that time he helped the local high school coach Arville Holmes. Holmes coached in a conservative manner, often winning low scoring affairs. He would even punt on third down occasionally to surprise the opposition. Madison learned a lot from him during this brief period and used some of the plays Holmes ran when he later became a head coach.

After a year and a half, Madison decided to finish college at Troy State University in Troy, Alabama. He, Rachel, and Becky made the move. Without ever talking to a football coach, Madison showed up for practice, and said he wanted to play. It wasn't long before Troy State offered him a scholarship.

Troy is a college town in south Alabama, sixty miles southeast of Montgomery and 120 miles northeast of Madison's hometown of Atmore. It is located on territory that once belonged to the Creek Indians and was settled in the early 1830s. It was originally named Deer Stand Hill. The town was sparsely populated for decades until the first railroad track came through in the 1870s and the town increased from less than five hundred people to over three thousand in a decade. The college was established in 1887 and led to the town's further growth.

During spring practice ahead of the 1955 season, the local newspaper, the *Troy Messenger*, mentioned Madison as a newcomer who "has stood out at the signal calling post and will probably give returning lettermen James Harris and Buddy Ellerbee a run for their money at this all-important position."

By the fourth game of the season, Madison had taken over as quarterback when his Trojans faced a tough, unbeaten Jacksonville State squad. They lost 12–0. But according to the *Troy Messenger*, Madison "called his plays well, mixing in end sweeps, pitch outs, streaks, and passes that kept the big Jax line on its toes."

Things turned around for one week when they defeated South Georgia College. Once again Madison started, but head coach Bill Clipson rotated three quarterbacks. The Red Wave closed out the season with three losses.

Heading into his senior season of 1956, Madison's teammates voted him team captain. His leadership ability was obvious to others at an early age, and he would lead young men for much of the next fifty years as a coach. But he still had one more season to play the game he loved.

Troy State opened against Livingston. Madison played well and led his team to a 21–6 win. The running game contributed greatly with the Red Wave rushing for 278 yards. Madison added another fifty-six yards passing on just four completions.

Losses to the University of Tampa, Delta State, and Jacksonville State followed the opening victory. Regarding the Jacksonville State loss, the *Troy Messenger* wrote that Madison "played probably his best game of the season and on one occasion romped forty yards for the longest run of Troy backs."

The next week, Troy State took on South Georgia College and their first-year head coach, Bobby Bowden, who eventually became one of the two winningest coaches in division one college football history with most of his success coming at Florida State. Bowden had left his alma mater, Howard College—now Samford University—where he had been an assistant coach for two years, to go to South Georgia as the athletic director, head football coach, head basketball coach, and head baseball coach. The Red Wave got back on track against South Georgia. Madison ran the opening kickoff of the second half to the South Georgia ten-yard line, which led to a touchdown in a 13–2 victory.

Troy State pulled out a thrilling 14–13 win over Austin Peay in their next contest, one of the biggest for Troy in quite a while, and head coach Bill Clipson was carried off the field by his players when the clock ran out. Unfortunately, it proved to be the final victory of the season. The Red Wave lost their final two games to Florence State and Carson-Newman.

With his playing career over, Carl Madison just needed to finish school so he could begin coaching. It wouldn't take long for that to become a reality. He got his first job at Carrabelle High School in Carrabelle, a tiny town in the Florida panhandle, located just east of Apalachicola at the mouth of the Carrabelle River on the Gulf of Mexico. It has been primarily a fishing village for decades, but from 1942–1946, it was the home of Camp Gordon Johnston where a quarter of a million infantrymen and their support units trained for amphibious operations.

The job opening in Carrabelle was for a football, baseball, and basketball coach and when Madison applied, he got the job coaching all three sports. Since he began in January, basketball was the first sport he coached, and he guided the team to a winning record. During that first basketball season, something occurred which, if it happened today, would draw intense scrutiny.

As coach, Madison drove the team bus for games away from home. Cheerleaders were allowed to ride with the team at Carrabelle in the past, but Madison told the principal he didn't want cheerleaders on the team bus. After one game in Bristol, Florida, the team ate dinner at a catfish restaurant. When Madison boarded the bus after the meal, he saw some heads duck down.

He announced, "Alright, if you're not supposed to be on the bus, get off."

No one got off. He said the same thing again, and still no one got off the bus.

Madison drove for a while, and eventually the heads popped up again. He stopped the bus, turned on the lights, and walked down the aisle to find three girls. He immediately ordered the three girls off the bus and left them on the side of the road while he drove away.

"Never did it enter my mind what could happen to them," Madison reflected. "I didn't even think anything about it."

The next day the principal came to see Madison and asked him what happened.

"I didn't take the girls to the game and didn't want the responsibility of getting them back home."

Madison received no punishment for the incident. He had punishment in store for the three boys who invited the girls onto the bus though—running one hundred laps to pay for their lapse in judgment.

"We won't run laps," said one boy, and the others agreed. "We'll quit the basketball team if you try and make us."

"Well, boys, if you quit basketball, you won't be allowed to play baseball either," Madison replied, knowing that all three boys were better baseball players than basketball players. "Don't make your decision right now. Take a day and think about it."

The next day, one of the boy's fathers was waiting for Madison when he arrived at school. "I don't think my boy will run the laps," he said.

"Well, I really hate that," Madison responded, "because if he doesn't run, he's not going to play baseball."

The boys showed up later in the day and still intended to quit.

"Take another day and think about it," Madison suggested.

Finally, on the day of the next ballgame, the boys decided to run the laps.

During the baseball season, Madison took his team to play against Apalachicola. Apalachicola High School's baseball field was lighted. Madison's Carrabelle team had never played under lights, and it showed when the Apalachicola pitcher threw a no-hitter against Carrabelle. Madison determined he would never play another team on terms like that again. He spent the rest of his coaching days doing all he could to ensure at least a level playing field for his young men, if not one tilted slightly in their favor.

That summer, Madison received an offer of an assistant coaching position at Tate High School, which he accepted, but before school started, the principal at Ernest Ward High in Walnut Hill contacted him. He wanted Madison as the head football coach there. Madison explained to him that he had already accepted the position at Tate. The principal told him he could get him out of that contract, which he did. Madison then became the head coach at Ernest Ward, while his brother Charlie took the job at Tate.

CHAPTER TWO

GETTING ESTABLISHED

WALNUT HILL IS an unincorporated community of less than
three thousand people in north Escambia County, Florida.
Though pecan trees are more dominant than walnut ones now, at one
time walnut trees were the most prevalent in the area and the reason for
the community being given its name. The first school in Walnut Hill was
established in 1886. A six-room school was eventually built in 1921 and
named for Ernest Ward, who had been a key individual in organizing a
school consolidation petition.

In the late 1950s at Ernest Ward, Madison coached football for
three years without assistant coaches. He credits that experience with
helping him understand football better. It forced him to learn offensive
line play and blocking schemes. It convinced him that success in football really came from effective play on the line of scrimmage, where the
bigger boys blocked, tackled, and went to battle at every snap of the ball.
There can be no question that coaching without assistants contributed to
the impressive organizational and time management skills he displayed
throughout his career. If he was going to achieve success, he simply had
to master those areas.

From his early days as a coach through the end of his career, players
much larger than Madison feared him. From your first introduction to

him you knew that you did not want to cross the man. If you did—either through disregarding instructions or indicating displeasure in any way towards what he told you—the results would not be pleasant. Your feelings on the matter held no sway with Madison. Virtually everything he said, all the directions he gave on the practice field or during games, was done with emphasis. He was not the calm, quiet conversation type. His manner of getting his message across was typically to yell it, often six inches or less from a player's face—and sometimes with his fingers grasping the player's facemask. This approach left little room for misinterpretation.

Not everyone approved of his methods, but Madison was not a tyrant. He wanted his players to perform at their absolute highest level, and he wanted them to succeed on and off the field. The vast majority of those who played for him over the years recognized this and were grateful. For some, this appreciation did not come until after their playing days ended.

He believed coaching young men carried an incredible responsibility that too many in the profession didn't understand. In his opinion, they just wanted *Coach* attached to their names. He felt they shouldn't have those positions because they were not there to develop the kids morally and physically. From the very beginning, Madison wanted to win, but he also wanted to make a difference in young men's lives.

Many years later, after being forced out at Tate High School, the first point of his resignation letter did not address his success on the field but spoke of how those who played for him "left with improved bodies and more confident minds."

The winning part didn't come immediately. In his first season at Ernest Ward, Madison's team won three games, lost six, and tied one. Among the losses was one in his hometown of Atmore to his old high school by a score of 45–0.

He later said, "That was an experience you don't forget. Getting embarrassed in your hometown like that. But I learned from it."

It proved to be one of the first of many lessons for Madison in his coaching career. What made him so successful in his profession was that he was constantly in learning mode. He never held to the theory that he had it all figured out. He also didn't want to be predictable. Many a football coach has experienced short-term success but was unable to sustain it because they could not adapt to changing circumstances. That was never the case with Carl Madison.

In his second season at Ernest Ward, the team returned only eight lettermen from the prior year, and the results were similar to 1957. The Eagles finished 4–5. But in his third year, Madison led the team to eight victories against just two defeats. That season's success caught the attention of Milton High School, who was looking for a new head football coach. Hiram Cook was a local businessman originally from Atmore who had some influence at Milton. He helped facilitate a transition, and Madison eventually received an offer he could not turn down.

The city of Milton is the county seat of Santa Rosa County and has a population of over ten thousand, though in 1960 it had just over four thousand residents. Located in the panhandle and incorporated in 1884, it is one of the oldest cities in Florida. The Blackwater River runs along its eastern edge and has provided the local population and visitors with boating, fishing, camping, and numerous outdoor activities for generations. Milton is also the home of Whiting Field, the largest air wing in the U.S. Navy. The high school was established in 1915 and over its one hundred year-plus history has grown to over eighteen hundred students.

When Carl Madison arrived at Milton, he had to make a big adjustment. While at Ernest Ward, he was the only coach. Now he could rely on assistants to help him with the team.

"I didn't know what to do with assistant coaches," he later commented.

Eventually, he learned how he could best utilize them, and throughout his career, he employed some extremely talented assistant coaches.

One of the coaches Madison hired was Floyd Adams. He was familiar with Adams from his days in Atmore as a youth. Upon graduating from Atmore High School, Adams went on to play baseball at Auburn and Howard College. He then joined the National Guard before finishing in 1959 when he began coaching in Springville, Alabama.

Madison contacted Adams about a coaching opening at Chumuckla. He suggested Adams apply for the job. Adams applied and then interviewed for it, but shortly after he returned home, he received another call from Madison saying he now needed an assistant ninth grade football coach and B-team basketball coach.

Adams accepted and later said of it, "That job was the best thing that ever happened to me, to get around a coaching staff that was that knowledgeable and had that much experience."

Madison faced a tremendous challenge with the 1960 Panther squad. He inherited a very young team with only five returning lettermen from a squad that went 5-4-1 in 1959. Fifteen of the thirty-three players on the roster were sophomores. The Panthers' largest starter was 190 pounds, and no other starter weighed more than 170 pounds.

"With a lot of hustle, we plan to battle to the whistle and hope to keep from being humiliated at the end," Madison commented.

Mickey Broxson was a junior at Milton High School when Madison arrived. His father died a couple of years before he started high school, and his mother worked to provide a decent living for the family. Broxson lived in Holley, about eighteen miles away, but at the time, Milton was the closest school, and he rose very early each morning to catch the bus. Because he stayed after school for football practice, no bus could take him home, so Broxson hitchhiked his way back to Holley most evenings. A local gentleman who worked at the meat market got off at 8:00 every night and drove by the school to see if Mickey had gotten a ride home. If not, the man picked up Broxson and drove him home.

When Broxson finally got his driver's license, the Milton High Quarterback Club provided him with gas money so he could afford to get from home to school and back each day. No doubt this was done with encouragement from Madison.

Broxson saw an immediate difference between Madison and the previous coach Phil Woodard. "Woodard was a tough guy, but he didn't say much. Madison was more involved with the players. God he was mean," Broxson later said.

The day Madison arrived, he required the boys on the team to do multiple hours of calisthenics. He got down on the ground with them and yelled into their faces. Many of the boys quit that day according to Broxson. "I reckon he wanted to set an example. And believe me, he did."

Broxson's thoughts regarding Madison reflect what many who played for him over the years would say. He was tough and could certainly be perceived as mean on many occasions. Though the yelling was intimidating, and you never wanted to be the recipient of his wrath, it was probably more the look that came with it that scared you the most. He could stare a hole through you. His eyes would squint. His jaw would harden, and you felt as though you and he were the only two people on the field. You knew he was about to erupt.

Everyone else typically froze to watch what was about to take place. Sometimes it lasted just a few seconds, even if it felt like minutes. But it often went on for a while. It was never arbitrary though, and you typically knew you'd messed up and that all hell was about to break loose. It was never taken lightly, and some handled it better than others. Many did not handle it well at all and decided they had better things to do with their time than subject themselves to such perceived indignities. But you never heard anyone who chose to continue say that they regretted it, and most consider it a badge of honor that they played for the man.

Keith Leonard, who later played for and coached with Madison, summed up the typical feelings as "a little bit of fear and a whole lot of respect." By this Leonard meant that Madison's players went to great lengths to avoid having him upset with them. No one wanted to be singled out and have Madison's anger focused on them because it was not a pleasant experience. But few, if any, ever avoided such a situation if they played for him for a reasonable length of time. Living with the fear of facing his wrath encouraged one to do things the proper way.

What separated him and eventually made Madison one of the true greats was his confidence. He had the ability to spread that confidence through everybody in the program, whether it be the players, the student body, the principal, or the community, and it was contagious.

Leonard said, "You were confident because he was so confident."

Madison made his players feel like the best, smartest, and most prepared team taking the field every Friday night. And they almost always were.

On September 16, 1960, the same day that Soviet-led Communists began withdrawal from the Congo and Warren Spahn of the Milwaukee Braves threw a no-hitter against the Philadelphia Phillies, Carl Madison made his debut as head coach of the Milton Panthers. His team defeated Crestview 21–7. Quarterback John Spencer, whose inexperience worried Madison going into the season, played well and scored the first touchdown on a seventeen-yard run.

The following week saw Madison lose his first game as Panther coach in a 39–38 slugfest with the Quincy Tigers. The Panthers trailed 33–16 in the second half but mounted a furious rally to grab a 38–33 lead with six minutes left on a forty-yard run by Spencer, but they couldn't hang on. Quincy scored late to hand Milton a defeat.

In a phone conversation with the *Pensacola News Journal,* Quincy coach Carlos Deason said game films showed the Panthers scored two of their touchdowns by using an "illegal center-sneak." Deason went on to claim that Milton ran the play five times and gained "about 180 or 190 yards."

In fact, Madison had his team run the center sneak multiple times. He moved one of the halfbacks to the center position and the center to right guard. Mickey Broxson was the fullback and had the responsibility of checking to see where the back judge lined up so he could position himself in front of him, making the official unable to tell what was going on. The halfback—now called *center*—would snap the ball but pull it up into his gut. The quarterback would fake a handoff to the right side, and everyone would run around the right end. The center stayed in place, counted *1,001 . . .1,002 . . .* and then took off to the left.

The official told the boys he had never seen a team fake so well, and he had no idea where the ball was. The Milton players bit their tongues.

Madison commented, "Apparently there was nothing illegal about the play. The officials never called it back, and we must have run it a half dozen times. They were approved Florida High School Activities Association officials and hired by Coach Deason."

Madison felt that Quincy was the primary beneficiary of the officiating. He pointed out that Milton was penalized thirty yards in the Tigers' game-winning drive and said, "Coach Deason was calling a lot of penalties from the sideline."

Madison later admitted to running a player off the sideline to try and catch a pass at the end of the contest. He told Panther receiver, H.S. Bohannon, to position himself among the cheerleaders, and when the ball was snapped, run onto the field. It sounded good in theory, but the team couldn't execute, and Milton fell just short of a huge victory.

Running Bohannan off the sideline and the center sneaks were illegal, and Madison knew it. He played the odds of not getting caught, which coaches throughout the history of the game have done in one form or another, but he admitted the Quincy loss was one of a handful that stuck with him.

Victories over Tate and Port St. Joe preceded losses to Marianna and Choctawhatchee, or *Choctaw* as it is primarily referred to by most people in the area. That left the Panthers 3–3. Madison wanted to prove to any doubters that Milton made the right choice in hiring him, and he was determined to do anything necessary to secure a winning season for his young team.

Midway through the 1960 season, Milton elected to withdraw from the West Florida Conference which included Choctawhatchee, Crestview, Tate, and Pensacola Catholic. The Panthers became part of the newly formed Northwest Florida Football Conference. The new conference included Quincy, Marianna, Port St. Joe, Defuniak Springs Walton, and Chipley.

The Panthers took on Catholic High in their next contest. They raced to a 28–0 halftime lead on their way to beating the Crusaders

48–6. Milton won their final three games to finish the season 7–3. Considering the youth of the team, the outlook was bright for the future of Panther football.

Madison's 1961 Panther football team entered the season "shy on experience and light in weight," according to the *Pensacola News Journal*. The team had thirty-eight members but only seven seniors. The heaviest player on the team was center Helge Swanson, at 185 pounds.

Still, Madison felt confident. "If we don't get anybody hurt, we'll give everybody a good game. It's hard for us to tell yet what we'll have. We have much work yet to do," he said.

The season opener found the Panthers facing Pensacola Tech and their new coach, Charlie Stokes, who went on to be superintendent of the Escambia County Schools for many years. Stokes felt that Milton was out of Tech's league.

Madison responded, "Well, I wish he was right, but he's not. I expect Tech to have a heckuva good ball club."

Stokes proved prophetic when Milton won the opener 42–12.

Milton hosted Quincy next. This time center sneaks were unnecessary, and unlike the year before, it was without controversy. The Panthers won a hard-fought battle, but a loss to Tate followed. The Aggie's touchdowns came from Clifford Walraven and Eddie Halfacre, both of whom later had sons play for Carl Madison during his Tate tenure.

The Panthers traveled to Port St. Joe the next week. Mickey Broxson helped them get back on track scoring four times in a 30–13 defeat of the Sharks. But the game still bothered Madison over forty years later. With the Panthers up big, he instructed his second team defense not to tackle the Port St. Joe runner and allow him to score. At the time, he thought it would help the confidence of Port St. Joe but realized afterwards that it ultimately embarrassed both squads.

"I never should have done that," Madison said.

Milton beat Marianna before suffering losses to Choctaw and W.S. Neal. Despite an overall record of 4–3, they remained 3–0 in league play. They won their final three games and clinched the conference championship in the finale against Chipley.

"It's not hard to win with this team spirit and fine coaching staff," Madison said. At just thirty years of age, he had established himself as one of the top coaches in the panhandle.

Upon the completion of the season, *Pensacola News* published a story that said the Florida High School Activities Association banned Milton from playing any postseason game due to alleged profanity used by Madison against an official earlier in the season in their contest with Tate. In addition, Madison received a $180 fine for investigation expenses.

Milton principal, Dr. John Southwell, defended his coach. He said he thought the officiating was poor during the Tate contest, and after looking at the films, he no longer had any doubt. Though the entire experience was unpleasant for Madison, it meant something to him for his principal to defend him the way Southwell had. Having strong relationships with those in positions of authority where he coached would be extremely important to him throughout his career.

During the early 1960s, high school football teams began filming their games and started the practice of swapping those films with their opponents the week before they played each other. That was how they scouted each other and looked for weaknesses or play tendencies, anything that might aid them in their preparation. Until that point, the larger schools relied strictly on sending an assistant coach or someone affiliated with the program to go watch future opponents' games and report what they saw. It was impossible to pick up on everything that way, and without assistants while at Ernest Ward, Madison couldn't glean much information about opposing teams. Fortunately, most of the teams his Ernest Ward squad played in those days ran either the T formation or double wing,[2] so he at least knew the basics of what to prepare for. Having film available to watch was a godsend to Madison.

---

2   A T formation consists of three running backs lined up side by side behind the center and the quarterback to form the shape of the letter T. A double wing is formed when two tight ends with two wingbacks lined up behind their outside shoulders along with a fullback lined up behind the quarterback.

The year 1962 was pivotal to the career of Carl Madison. He began a three-year stretch where the perception of him went from being just a good high school football coach to someone who had the capability of building a powerhouse program. That is what he desired—not just a team that experienced better than average success, but a program that could always be counted on to win at a high level and compete for championships.

Headed into the 1962 season, local coaches chose Milton as the conference favorites again. Plenty of key players returned, including all-conference tackle Fred Hudson and Helge Swanson at center. Madison told the Milton Lion's Club that this group would go undefeated. It was a bold statement given he had never coached a team to a season with fewer than two losses. However, he was particularly confident not only in his team but in his own ability as a coach to guide them. Most coaches would shudder at the prospect of placing that kind of pressure on themselves.

Carl Madison was not most coaches.

The Panthers won their opener 40–0 against Pensacola Tech before facing Quincy in what most thought would decide the conference champion. Quincy had not lost since their early season defeat by the Panthers the previous year and received two of the six first place votes in the preseason coaches' poll. In another 40–0 victory, eight different Panther players scored touchdowns.

Wins over Tate, Port St. Joe, and Marianna followed before the Panthers faced the higher classification (AA) Choctawhatchee Indians in a contest the *Pensacola News Journal* dubbed the "Game of the Week."

"We will have to play one of our better games if we are to win," Madison said.

Milton jumped on top early on a Winston Norris touchdown only to see the Indians tie the score in the second quarter. Wayne Smith scored before the half as Milton took a 13–6 lead into the locker room. Choctaw cut the lead to 13–12 in the third quarter, but Wayne Smith ran for two touchdowns of more than sixty yards in the fourth quarter, and the Panthers remained unbeaten, 27–12.

A win over W.S. Neal came next, and for the Panthers' game against Catholic, Madison employed the somewhat novel concept of starting players either on offense or defense. None would start on both sides of the ball.

"We think our boys will give a better performance playing only offense rather than both ways," Madison stated.

While he may not have been the very first to implement the "two-platoon system" as it was called, it was by no means the common practice of the time. In fact, it was not allowed in college football from 1954–1964. The system proved successful as Milton's defense held the Catholic offense to a total of fifty-four yards in a dominating victory.

Milton then had an opportunity to secure the Northwest Florida Conference championship against Defuniak Springs, Walton. After a slow start, they cruised 42–6 and the conference championship belonged to the Panthers for the second consecutive year.

All that remained was a final game against Chipley and an opportunity for an unbeaten season. Milton jumped out to a 20–0 first quarter lead on their way to a 60–0 victory. Wayne Smith found the endzone three times making him the leading scorer in northwest Florida football with a record 158 points.

In their undefeated 1962 season, Madison's Panthers outscored their opponents 410–76 and finished the year ranked eleventh in the state of Florida in the *Miami Herald* high school football poll. Madison's decision to employ a two-platoon system that year proved to be a wise one. No Florida High School football playoffs occurred in 1962—they did not begin until the following year—and thus no opportunity to prove how truly strong they were, but by all measures the team was an extraordinary one.

Before the 1963 season, the consensus was that Milton would dominate the Northwest Florida Football Conference. In the coaches' poll, they were selected unanimously as the top team. The Panthers came into the season on a thirteen-game winning streak. Wayne Smith, Sonny

Owens, and Greg McRanie combined to score thirty-one touchdowns in 1962—and all returned. The Milton offensive line averaged 175 pounds, undersized even by early 1960s high school football standards. The Panther backfield however, averaged 189 pounds per man with Smith and McRanie both tipping the scales at 195 pounds. An average coach might have succumbed to the temptation to put his larger players on the line, but Madison recognized things others couldn't. He would go decades winning with undersized linemen because he taught them outstanding techniques and utilized the quickness of so many of them.

Milton opened the 1963 season against Quincy and won handily. Tate came next with an opportunity for the Panthers to win for the fifteenth consecutive time.

Aggie coach Ralph Chaudron commented ahead of the matchup, "Milton will be as tough as any team we will play this season and from the scouting reports they are big and fast."

It was a challenge for the Panthers, but they prevailed 25–22.

Wins over Port St. Joe and Mobile McGill led into a huge matchup with Choctawhatchee for the second consecutive year. The Indians were ranked sixth in the state while Milton sat at seventh. It was almost a foregone conclusion that the Panthers would be conference champions, so the contest with the Indians provided an opportunity to see how they matched up against one of the larger schools in the state. Choctaw came in with an unblemished 3–0 record.

Things started well for the Panthers when Choctaw's bad snap on a first quarter punt led to a Ricky Wiggins touchdown. Wayne Smith scored on runs of two and twenty-three yards in the second quarter increasing the advantage to 19–0. It stayed that way through the third before the teams traded fourth quarter scores. When the final whistle blew, the Panthers had a convincing 32–14 win and with it they moved to number five in the state rankings.

Milton beat Crestview 42–0 for their nineteenth consecutive victory. Then came Marianna, also unbeaten at 5–0. Milton got off to a great start when Wayne Smith went seventy yards for a touchdown just a minute and twenty seconds in. But the Bulldogs responded with a drive of their own, and when they scored again in the second quarter, they held a 13–7 lead. It was only the second time all season the Panthers trailed. It took Milton just four plays to rectify the situation when Sonny Owens went thirty-four yards to tie the score at 13–13 going into halftime. Second half scoring runs by Wayne Smith and Ricky Wiggins sealed things for the Panthers as they escaped with another victory.

The Panthers won their twenty-first straight game and clinched the Northwest Florida Conference championship against Defuniak Springs Walton. Milton followed that with a 41–0 drubbing of Tallahassee Florida High that gave them their third straight Northwest Florida Conference championship. Madison rewarded his squad by allowing them to stay the night in Tallahassee and see Florida State host North Carolina State the next day at Doak Campbell Stadium. They got to watch their former Panther teammate Helge Swanson start at center for the Seminoles when they defeated the Wolfpack 14–0.

The Panthers faced a much larger school in the regular season finale of 1963 when they took on Dothan (AL) High School.

"We'll win," Madison stated.

"Don't take us for granted," Dothan head coach Charlie McCall said.

McCall admitted that they didn't realize how tough Milton was when they scheduled them. The game was played in the evening after word came earlier in the day that President John F. Kennedy had been assassinated. All over the country decisions were made whether to go forward with sporting events. The American Football League postponed their weekend football contests, while the NFL chose to play their seven scheduled games. Numerous college games were postponed, including the annual Harvard-Yale matchup, given Harvard was Kennedy's alma mater.

But Florida High schools went ahead with their scheduled games. Milton only completed one pass the entire evening but walked away victorious 20–0, their twenty-third consecutive victory, matching a streak by Pensacola High from 1957–1960. The Panthers moved to number three in the *Miami Herald* state rankings.

Madison stated, "I think we are just as good as any team in the state, and we thought we could beat any team on our schedule and did." His confidence shone through once again; it was never an act for him. He just had it, and because he did, his players did too.

State football playoffs began in Florida in 1963, but there was no opportunity for an A classification school to compete in them. Fortunately, after the completion of their regular season, Milton received an invitation to play in the Meninak Bowl in Jacksonville, Florida against a much larger Jacksonville Jackson High School. Jackson had only one loss on the season but three ties.

Madison discussed his team's travel plans. "We'll beat 'em on Friday and travel home Saturday," he said.

The matchup would be a challenge for the Panthers and their running game. The Jackson defensive front was huge by the standards of the day. Across the line they went 215, 215, 210, 195, and 195 pounds, outweighing their counterparts on the offensive line of Milton by over thirty pounds on average.

By kickoff, it had been three weeks since the Panthers last played. Jackson scored early to take the lead, and the teams battled closely for the remainder of the night. Milton scored with 2:40 left to play to tie the score 13–13, but the Panthers' ensuing kickoff sailed out of bounds, and Jackson took over on their own forty-yard line. They proceeded to march down the field on a drive that culminated in a touchdown with just twenty-nine seconds left to play. Milton could not manage to do anything in the remaining time, and Jackson prevailed 19–13.

Madison considered Jackson the best team they played all season. "A lot better than I expected," he said afterwards. Regarding the end of the team's 23-game win streak, he commented, "I guess we'll just have to start over again next year."

There is little doubt that Milton would have been Florida Class A state champions if such a thing existed in 1963. They were the only A team ranked in the top ten throughout the season or who even received votes. Carl Madison was named Northwest Florida Coach of the Year by the *Pensacola News Journal* for the job he did that season.

Carl Madison loved coaching. "I've always wanted to be a coach, and I could coach this game of football twelve months a year if they played it that long," he once said.

By 1964, he had seven years head coaching experience. In May of that year, he shocked the school and community when he announced his resignation from Milton to take a job at McArthur High School in Hollywood, Florida.

Milton principal John Southwell stated, "We're trying to get him to reconsider, and if he changes his mind, we'll ask the board to rescind his resignation."

Madison told the *Pensacola News Journal* that the decision wasn't final and that "if two or three things were worked out," he'd reconsider the move, but he did not elaborate on what those things were. It took a little time, but things were resolved to his satisfaction and Madison remained the Panther head coach.

Coming off consecutive unbeaten regular seasons, the 1964 Milton team did not lack confidence, but it did lack experience since ten of the eleven offensive starters from the prior year had graduated. The players were part of an established program now, and they expected to be able to fill in as prior players had done when their turn came. You could be certain that Carl Madison continued to expect success.

The Panthers opened the season against Lafayette, Georgia and won 21–6, and for the first time in memory, a Madison offense saw more passing yards (102) than rushing (101). This was an early indication of the type of coach Madison was. Although he always believed in establishing the run and primarily relied on it with most of his teams, he could adapt a game plan to whatever he felt was necessary to win. If his team needed to pass more, they would be prepared for that as well. When looking through the lens of modern offensive football, one might question his team accumulating just over two hundred yards of total offense, but it was a different game back then. Plus, he had the luxury of fielding a defense that allowed just twenty total yards in the contest with Lafayette.

A 19–0 defeat of Tate preceded a tie with Mobile McGill High.[3]

"We made too many mistakes to beat McGill. Our defense played real well after the first quarter, but our offense never got started," Madison said.

The long Panther regular season winning streak ended at twenty-four but an unbeaten one remained.

Wins over Choctawhatchee and Crestview stretched the unbeaten streak to twenty-seven. Then came a matchup with Marianna. The Bulldogs looked for revenge after suffering their only defeat to Milton the prior year. Marianna was only 2–2 on the season but still figured to be tough. Marianna posted first and second quarter scores on their way to a 13–0 halftime lead. Milton rallied with two third quarter scores on runs from Miller and Kembro, but neither team could find paydirt in the fourth quarter and the game ended in a 13–13 tie. The tie left them with an overall record of 4-0-2, but more importantly, a 1-0-1 record in the district. They still held their conference title destiny in their hands.

The matchup with Defuniak Springs Walton would likely decide the Northwest Florida Conference championship.

"This is the biggest game of the year for us," Walton coach Buddy Supple said ahead of the matchup.

Madison stated, "Our boys should want this more than any game so far this season."

More than eighty-five hundred fans showed up at Milton and witnessed the Panthers fall behind in the first quarter 7–0. Milton answered with a touchdown in the second quarter, but a failed conversion kept the score at 7–6. Both teams added scores in the second half, but a Kenny Kembro pass was intercepted in the waning seconds and Milton fell 14–13. The unbeaten regular season streak that dated back to 1962 ended as did likely any hope for a conference championship.

---

3   Overtime periods to settle ties in Florida high school football did not begin until the 1970s.

The following week, the Panthers thrashed Tallahassee Florida High 34–7. But in one of the most uninspiring performances by a Milton team during Madison's tenure, the Panthers lost 36–3 to Dothan in their next game.

Milton travelled to Niceville for their final contest of the 1964 campaign. Although there wasn't much to play for from the Panthers perspective, the Eagles still had an opportunity to be conference champions. If Milton could not win it, they certainly didn't want someone else doing so at their expense. They took care of the Niceville title hopes by handing them a 27–13 defeat.

By many standards, a 6-2-2 season was successful, but considering Milton had won twenty-three consecutive regular season games and was three-time defending conference champions coming into the 1964 season, it left a somewhat bitter taste. Carl Madison did not have time to sit around bemoaning a "down season," though. He would regroup and begin planning for the 1965 campaign. The adversity of a less-than-stellar campaign would pale in comparison to later challenges, but coaches are often measured by how they respond to setbacks.

Going into the 1965 season, Carl Madison felt like his team would have their strongest passing attack in years. "We've got a couple of boys who can throw the ball, and that will really help your ground game," he commented.

This was important. A good passing attack forces the defense to commit to playing deeper and covering receivers, which opens things up on the line of scrimmage and gives the running game better opportunities. Conversely, a strong running game forces the defense to commit more players closer to the line and frees things up for the passing game. Most good coaches want to achieve the type of balance between running and passing that causes problems for defenses in that they have to try to defend both on virtually every play.

Madison was that kind of coach.

Milton opened the 1965 season with the same opponent it began with in 1964: Lafayette, Georgia. Milton throttled them 34–0. Wins over Pensacola Catholic and Tate followed before the 3–0 Panthers took on the 2-0-2 Choctaw Indians.

"They're big and strong, and those two boys, [Larry] Williamson and [Duff] Maki are two of the finest football players I've seen this year," Madison said.

Madison was correct in his assessment of Larry Williamson. The Indian quarterback threw for two scores and ran for another in a 21–13 Choctaw victory.

The Panthers defeated Crestview and Marianna before traveling to Defuniak Springs Walton with an opportunity to clinch the conference crown. The Braves ended the Panthers long regular season unbeaten streak the prior year in a thrilling 14–13 contest. Kenny Kembro broke away for a seventy-nine-yard score in the first quarter, and Milton led 7–0 at the half. Rodney Griffis tacked on a third quarter touchdown, and John Willey rounded out the scoring. The Panthers defeated the Braves 21–0, making them Northwest Florida Conference champions for the fourth time in five years.

Milton closed out the season by defeating Niceville 47–0. It capped a nice 7–1 comeback season from the "disappointing" 6-2-2 record of 1964. Madison once again garnered Northwest Florida Coach of the Year honors, while John Willey was named the Player of the Year, the first Milton player to receive the honor.

Despite the team and individual successes, all was not well. The fact that Milton only played eight games concerned Madison greatly. He had a difficult time finding teams to play the Panthers.

Legendary Tallahassee Leon coach Gene Cox recalled Madison jumping up on a table at a coaches' meeting and yelling, "I'll play anybody, anywhere."

Unfortunately, he wasn't getting enough takers. The point system worked against Milton, making it difficult for them to advance to the state playoffs—another sore spot for Madison. It rewarded the larger schools and those who played more games, things beyond Madison's control. That kept a very deserving 1965 Panther team from participating in the state playoffs, especially frustrating given that the Litkenhous ratings listed them as the second-best A classification team in Florida.

So, when John Perry, the principal of Milton who served as an assistant coach when he first arrived, decided to leave the school, Madison figured he should consider moving on as well. He started exploring other options and looked towards Georgia as a potential landing spot.

In July, Carl Madison announced his resignation from Milton and said he was taking over as head football coach and athletic director at Forest Park High School in Georgia.

Al Padgett of the *Pensacola News Journal* wrote of his departure, "Our section lost an outstanding coach when Carl Madison left Milton in favor of Forest Park, GA. Carl isn't the best public relations man I ever saw, but he sure has a way of winning football games."

Forest Park High School is an Atlanta-area school approximately fifteen miles south of downtown. It was established in 1928 and is one of Clayton County's oldest high schools. In 1966, it needed a new head football coach. The team won just three games in 1965 and had only managed one winning season in the previous six years. They desperately needed new leadership to help turn things around. During their search for a person to lead them in a new direction, they came across a Madison from northwest Florida who seemed to fit the bill, but it was Charlie, Carl's brother, to whom they initially offered the job.

Charlie turned down their offer to stay closer to home at Tate.

Carl Madison took a trip to the mountains that summer and thought he would just drop by the school to speak with them. As Madison sat in the office waiting, he couldn't help but overhear a conversation between the principal and the mother of one of the school's students. The student appeared to have a discipline problem, and Madison was extremely impressed with the firm manner in which the principal handled the conversation.

That's someone I would enjoy working for, he thought. By the time he left Atlanta, a deal was in place for him to be the next head football coach of Forest Park. He began working there on August 1, 1966.

When Carl Madison arrived at Forest Park, he had already established himself as a very successful high school football coach. He maintained certain philosophies that he would not sacrifice because he valued
long-term, sustainable success over immediate results. Fairness was important to him.

Though few players during their time with Madison suspected he
possessed a sensitive side, in fact, he did. When his coaching days concluded, he said, "I believed in treating all the kids the same regardless of
where you came from or who you were. There were special [players], but
nobody knew. I would have liked to have said 'Man, I really like you,' but
I didn't. I wanted to a lot of times."

His emphasis on attention to detail and perfect execution were re-
curring themes. In practice during the running of a play, if just one player
out of eleven did not execute properly, that alone was enough to rerun
the play. If that player corrected his mistake but another one didn't do his
job correctly on the second go round, the result would be the same. Run
it again. This went on for as many times as it took for everyone to execute
perfectly. It often took five or more times for that to occur.

A common misconception among opposing teams and casual fans
was that Madison's playbooks included many plays, but that wasn't the
case. Throughout his coaching days he had a few basic plays, but many
of them included multiple options. The quarterback needed to read the
defense properly and make decisions whether to hand the ball off to the
lead back, keep it, or pitch to the trailing back. The key to his teams' success was their ability to execute those plays with great precision because
of how they practiced.

Forest Park was nicknamed the Panthers, the same as Madison's
Milton team. In a high school of approximately seventeen hundred students, only thirty young men played football when Carl Madison took
over the program. Of those thirty, only five—Dwight Peppers, Mike
Jenkins, Tommy Hutto, Tommy Burge, and Dennis McCollum—had
seen action on the varsity squad the previous year. Madison essentially
started from scratch, and it would not be a quick fix.

On September 2, 1966, Carl Madison made his debut at Forest Park against the Eagles of North Clayton. After falling behind 6–0 in the first quarter, Dwight Pepper threw a couple of touchdown passes, and Forest Park cruised to a 27–12 victory, giving Madison his first high school win as a head coach in the state of Georgia.

Any thoughts that Madison was a miracle worker and that everything would go smoothly from then on dissipated the next week when the Panthers fell behind North Fulton 28–0 at the half on their way to a 62–33 defeat.

Against lesser competition, but just a week after giving up sixty-two points, the Panther defense shut out Jonesboro in a 21–0 Forest Park victory. The Panthers ran their record to 3–1 the following week, matching their victory total from the entire 1965 season. After falling behind Grady High School, Forest Park rallied to win 14–7 with Pat Turner's five-yard touchdown run in the fourth quarter proving to be the difference.

Consecutive losses came next, but defeats of Woodward Academy and Therrell High moved Forest Park to 5–3 in the season and meant a victory in either of their final two contests would give them a winning season. That wasn't to be as they fell to perennial power and unbeaten Robert E. Lee, then again in their season finale to Tucker. A 5–5 season was an improvement over 1965, but it fell short of Madison's expectations.

Forest Park supporters were ecstatic when they hired Carl Madison from Milton. After compiling a 48-9-2 record at the Florida school, they believed he would provide the same results along with a Georgia state championship.

Ray Tapley of the *Atlanta Constitution* asked Madison if this was the year for a state championship at Forest Park.

"Good heavens no," Madison replied. "If we ever have a state title team, it certainly won't be this year. We're much too inexperienced. Why, we only have thirteen lettermen, and only five of our thirteen seniors have ever played ball before. Also, we have a total of only forty-seven boys out for all the teams, and that's much too small for a school the size of ours."

Madison knew what kind of team he had and wanted to temper expectations—and not just of the media but the Forest Park community. Throughout his career, he wasn't bashful about saying he had a strong team if he believed it were true. He also wasn't afraid to tell people when the opposite was the case.

The results of the 1967 season proved Madison's initial assessment accurate. His group wasn't yet ready to compete for championships. They tied the opener with North Clayton before posting wins against North Fulton, Jonesboro, and Grady giving them a 3-1-1 record at the half-way point of the season. After defeating Southwest, things looked very promising, but then the wheels came off. A 20–13 loss to Woodward Academy began a streak of four straight losses to end the season, resulting in a final record of 4-5-1 and giving Madison his first losing season since his second one at Ernest Ward.

CHAPTER THREE

ASCENDENCY

WITH THE REALIGNMENT of conferences in 1968, Forest Park found themselves in a new region: 7-AAA. A preseason article in the *Atlanta Journal* proclaimed that there would be no more waiting until next year.

"This is Next Year," it stated. "The contingent of football players boasts size, speed, depth, and experience. They have several of the finest interior lineman in the state and most important, they have had a full year of playing under Coach Madison's tutelage. Veteran observers are claiming that this could be the Panther team that goes all the way."

The Panthers opened the season against North Clayton in the new Tara Stadium which was built to host all high school games in Clayton County. With a seating capacity of eleven thousand spectators and a parking lot that held twenty-five hundred vehicles, it was considered the finest high school football facility in the state of Georgia. The two teams had tied the previous year with each coach believing he had the better squad.

The Panthers left no doubt in 1968. An estimated crowd of over eight thousand looked on as Jimmy Germany scored the first touchdown in the new stadium on a twenty-two-yard pass from Randy Kidd. Forest Park never looked back on their way to a 21–6 victory.

Next came Avondale. When Carl Madison came to Forest Park from Milton, some in the Atlanta area referred to him as the "Calvin Ramsey" of northwest Florida. Now he got to take on the real Calvin Ramsey and his Blue Devils. The home stadium of Avondale was known by the nickname "Death Valley." Avondale had only lost once since the stadium opened in 1958—a playoff game—and it had suffered only two regular season defeats since 1962.

Charlie Roberts of the *Atlanta Constitution* reported on the game. "A band of roving Panthers from Forest Park prowled into Avondale's 'Death Valley' and converted it into a death trap for the home-loving Blue Devils, who never before had been conquered in regular season in their never-neverland."

Touchdown passes from Kidd to Freddie Cash and Al Eubanks in the third quarter led the Panthers to a stunning 14–7 victory.

Avondale's coach, Calvin Ramsey, commented, "We just couldn't stop them. You gotta have the ball to win, and we never did get it. In the third quarter, I think we ran one series of plays."

Madison said, "I knew if we stayed close, or were tied at half, we'd beat them. Our boys just had to find out that they're [Blue Devils] not so damn tough."

It was a good lesson for his team. He could tell them in practice that they were good enough to play with the best teams in the state and hopefully they would believe it, but ultimately, they had to discover that for themselves on the playing field during games.

After the win over Avondale, the *Atlanta Constitution* named Forest Park its "Team of the Week," and the Panthers moved into the eighth position in the State AAA rankings.

The week leading up to the matchup with Towers High proved eventful. Madison was stricken on Wednesday with a kidney stone that required surgery on Friday afternoon, the day of the game. His wife Rachel sat in the press box and updated him by telephone, although she wasn't sure he comprehended all she said due to the anesthesia. Proving how well Madison trained his staff, Assistant Coach John Smith took over the coaching duties, and Forest Park didn't miss a beat, cruising 31–2.

By the time they faced Jonesboro, Forest Park ranked sixth in the *Atlanta Constitution* Georgia AAA rankings. The 0–3 Cardinals did not figure to be a tough matchup for Forest Park, even though Madison remained in the hospital recovering. When the Panthers scored early on an eighty-yard interception return by Doug Burnett, it seemed they would coast to another victory. But by the fourth quarter, they trailed 17–14. With the clock ticking down, the Panthers faced a third and twelve near mid-field. Dennis Sullivan took a handoff and fumbled the ball when hit, but it was picked out of the air by Jim Lyle, a 240-pound lineman who rambled for ten yards. On fourth and two, Bobby Slagle ran for twenty yards, and a couple of plays later, Kidd hit Terry Peeples for the winning score with 2:17 left on the clock.

Interviewed from his hospital room Madison said, "I was there in spirit, though. I was right there. I think they were too keyed up."

Victories over Walker, Columbia, Griffin, and Gordon ran the Panthers record to 8–0. Forest Park now ranked in the top five teams in the state, but the competition was about to get tougher.

The next to last game of the regular season came against a solid Clarkston team that sported a 6–2 record. Madison made sure the team did not look ahead to the matchup against Robert E. Lee. Randy Kidd suffered a leg injury, and Madison chose to hold him out in hopes that he'd recover in time to play against Lee. On a cold, rainy night, Dennis Sullivan helped pick up the slack of a missing Randy Kidd, running for one hundred yards while the Panthers cruised 24–7.

Across town in similar weather, Lee High School tied Avondale 0–0, ending their winning streak but still setting up a battle for the 7-AAA championship with Forest Park. The Panthers came in with a 9–0 record, while the Rebels of Robert E. Lee were 8-0-1.

The game took place at Robert E. Lee's home field in Clarkston. Their coach, Jim Cavan, was the dean of Georgia High School football coaches and in his thirty-first season. Forest Park had never beaten Lee in six tries nor had they ever scored on them.

After a scoreless first quarter, the Panthers started a possession on their own twenty-four-yard line in the second. Nothing but running plays got them to the Rebel thirty where Madison finally called for a passing play. Kidd hit an open Dennis Sullivan at the twenty-yard line, and he ran the rest of the way for the score. With 3:04 left in the half, Jeff King kicked a thirty-one-yard field goal to give the Panthers a 10–0 lead. The Rebels drove down the field to the Panther ten-yard line late in the half, but Tommy Hunt intercepted a pass to prevent a score. Forest Park took the 10–0 lead into halftime. The Panther defense stood strong in the second half until the final minute when Lee finally got on the scoreboard on a thirty-one-yard touchdown pass. Forest Park recovered the onside kick and ran out the clock for a 10–7 victory, making them region champs.

The Panthers traveled to play a once-beaten Athens team in the first round of the playoffs. The Trojans were "a fine team that hits hard and comes at you," according to Madison. Many of the Panther players were recovering from a bout with the flu. In front of six thousand fans, the Panthers took the opening kickoff and drove seventy-three yards on eleven plays with Jimmy Germany capping the drive with a score from six yards out. Things were never in doubt from there, and Forest Park advanced to the North State Finals.

The North State Finals took place at Tara Stadium against the Dalton Catamounts. Dalton was the AA Georgia state champions in 1967 and now in their first year in AAA. Their record was 10–1. Bobby Slagle had cracked ribs and was out, while Jimmy Germany battled the flu. Neither of these situations boded well for Forest Park.

In front of nine thousand fans, the Panthers jumped out to a 7–0 lead in the first quarter, and things stayed that way until the half. On the opening drive of the second half, Forest Park quarterback Randy Kidd saw Freddie Cash wide open and hit him with a pass that Cash took forty-five yards for a score. Dalton fumbled the subsequent kickoff, and the Panthers scored their third touchdown on a Kidd keeper. Forest Park added a score before Dalton finally managed to find the end zone. That wrapped up the scoring, and the Panthers advanced to the state championship with a 28–7 victory.

Forest Park faced Valdosta in the championship game. Valdosta was one of the traditional powers in Georgia High School football having won twelve state championships. The Wildcats were coached by Wright Bazemore, who the *Atlanta Journal* referred to as "the King of high school football in Georgia." Few could argue that assertion since Bazemore sported a record of 252 wins and forty-two losses. Valdosta was a dynasty in South Georgia. The young men who played there had been running the Valdosta system since the time they first put on pads as eight or nine year olds. The youth league in Lowndes County had been preparing them for high school football.

Although most of the attention focused on Bazemore and the Valdosta team, many recognized Carl Madison as a star in the making himself. Bill Hartigan wrote in the *Atlanta Constitution,* "We will probably see the two best coached teams of the year, or of any year, collide Saturday."

Valdosta came in unbeaten, the same as Forest Park. The Wildcats defense had only given up nineteen points in the entire season and none in the playoffs.

Still, Madison remained confident. "We think we'll whip 'em," he said. Though he did go on to state, "Our scouts have a lot of respect for them. They say they're the Green Bay Packers, the Baltimore Colts, and the Los Angeles Rams all rolled into one."

The temperature was twenty-four degrees at kickoff. Becky Madison, a young girl at the time, could still recall how cold it was almost forty years later. On the Panther's first possession, Dennis Sullivan fumbled, and the Wildcats recovered on Forest Park's thirty-seven. On Valdosta's first play, Larry Howell threw a touchdown pass to Mike Flail. Following the contest, Howell became the first African American to receive a scholarship to play football at Georgia Tech, signing the offer under the goal post. Three plays later, Randy Kidd fumbled, and a Valdosta defender picked the ball up and ran in for another score. The Panthers responded with a four play, eighty-yard drive. When Jeff King missed the extra point—his first miss of the season—the score stood at 14–6. Early in the second quarter, Dennis Sullivan ran in from four yards out and cut the lead to 14–12.

Unfortunately, those were the final points the Panthers scored. Late in the first half, Randy Kidd threw an interception, and Valdosta drove for another touchdown making it 21–12 at the break. The second half was all Valdosta. They added sixteen points to make the final score 37–12. It had been an unbelievable season for the Panthers. They achieved things never seen at Forest Park High School. Still, it was a time of disappointment for the players and coaches, as they fell short of their ultimate goal.

Madison summarized the contest. "This was not one of our better games. In fact, I believe it was our poorest game of the year. We just were not ready. Offensively and defensively, we didn't execute the plays, and you can't win if you don't execute."

Bazemore said of Forest Park, "They've got a real fine football team. They're well coached, and they do have a good running back. I don't know how good they really are; it was too cold there to tell."

In voting by fellow coaches, Madison edged out Wright Bazemore to become AAA Georgia Coach of the Year. He also received the High School Coach of the Year award from the Georgia Touchdown Club.

The world changed dramatically between the end of the 1968 season and the kickoff of 1969. Man landed on the moon over the summer of 1969, and Carl Madison took his mind off football to contemplate what a spectacular accomplishment that was. But just for a brief period. He had to prepare a football team for a year in which they would primarily be the hunted rather than the hunter.

After their success in 1968, people were naturally excited about the upcoming season. But with only twelve returning lettermen from the state runner up team, it was difficult to expect similar results.

"We have only four or five who started last year. But we've got a lot of boys who want to play," Carl Madison told the *Atlanta Constitution* before the beginning of the season. He went on to say, "Tradition will win a lot of ballgames. We'll need that too. Many, many times teams are beat because of tradition—they know the winning tradition the opposition has, and they are mentally beat before the game. If we can get a few of those kinds of wins, it'll help. But we won't be weak. No sir. We're planning on winning this thing [region 5-AAA] again."

His comments demonstrated how well Madison understood the mental side of the game. Physical talent played an extremely important role in success on the football field, but having the proper mindset was critical too. He emphasized the mental side of the game, and it played a large part in his success.

The opener went about as well as could be expected. Forest Park totaled over 450 yards of offense with new starting quarterback, Tommy Hunt, leading the attack. The Panther offense scored the first time they touched the ball and never looked back on their way to a 49–6 defeat of North Clayton.

Week two was an entirely different story against Avondale. Ten thousand fans showed up at Tara stadium to watch Forest Park take on the Blue Devils, but dreams of another victory and a second consecutive undefeated regular season soon came crashing down. Avondale scored twice in the opening five minutes, and though the Panthers answered with a second quarter score on a blocked punt, they never challenged and fell 34–7.

Madison's squad got back on track by beating Towers, Jonesboro, Walker, Columbia, and Griffin. The Panthers record stood at 6–1, and it appeared they had moved beyond the early season loss to Avondale.

A Forest Park-Clarkston battle between "two of Region 7-AAA's heavyweights" according to the *Atlanta Constitution*, came next. Madison's team employed a trick play on the opening kickoff. Bobby Slagle caught a lateral and raced ninety-five yards for a touchdown. The game seesawed until the Angoras scored in the final three minutes to beat the Panthers 21–17.

Forest Park faced their old nemesis Robert E. Lee High in the season finale. The Rebels no doubt had revenge on their mind after losing to the Panthers for the first time in their history the previous season. In 1968, neither team had suffered a defeat when they met, but this year each came in with seven wins and two losses. Lee ran their season record to 8–2 while dropping Forest Park to 7–3 with a 20–10 defeat of the Panthers.

It was another successful season for Carl Madison and the Forest Park Panthers though they fell short of the success experienced in 1968. While only returning a handful of starters, they won seven games and outscored their opponents 223 to eighty-nine. One only had to look back at the years before he arrived at Forest Park and the limited success they'd achieved to recognize that things were much different now. High expectations and a culture of winning had been established.

Charles McCord of the *Atlanta Constitution* referred to 1969 as a "building year" for Forest Park and expected them "jump back into the real thing in AAA" in 1970.

They weren't given the opportunity to ease into things. In recent years, the Panthers played Robert E. Lee High School late in the season, often the final game. In 1970, Forest Park opened against Jim Cavan's strong Rebel squad. McCord wrote that it should be "a real old fash-ion[ed] gridiron rhubarb." Bobby Slagle scored in the second quarter and the Panthers carried a 7–0 lead into the halftime locker room, but they couldn't hold on in the second half, falling 14–7.

The Panthers then rallied to whip Newton County 33–0 and appeared at number ten in the Georgia AAA rankings for their performance. Newnan came next, and the evening got off to a strange start when the Panthers showed up wearing the same color jerseys as their opponents.

Newnan head coach Max Boss said of the incident, "Hoss, we just gave 'em some of our white ones. Shoot, it wasn't a thing to get upset about."

It was a battle, but Forest Park fell 29–27.

The Panthers managed to even their record at 2–2 with a 32–0 win over Washington High then followed that up with by beating LaGrange and Jonesboro before falling to Griffin. It proved to be the last loss Madison suffered at Forest Park. Victories over Therrell, Price, and North Clayton wrapped up the season and gave the Panthers a final record of 7–3.

In February of 1971, the *Atlanta Constitution* reported that Madison, "after doing much thinking and mind changing the past three days, will become the new head football coach at Chamblee." Chamblee was another Atlanta-area high school, less than fifteen miles northeast of downtown.

Shortly after accepting the position, Madison experienced a change of heart. "I'm not going to Chamblee. Personal reasons, I guess you could say. I wrote out my resignation just last week and turned it in," he stated. He went on to say that he hoped to stay in the administrative or educational field and when asked if he would continue coaching responded, "I hope not. I'm not sure where I'll be next year."

The article that included those Madison quotes was from March 10. The March 4 edition of the *Pensacola News Journal* reported that he accepted the head football coach and athletic director position at Tate High School. There was obviously a lack of communication somewhere whether intended or not. But no matter the circumstances, Carl Madison returned to the Florida panhandle where most people believed he belonged. He would coach in the area for the next twenty-eight years.

Madison had proven he was a very talented football coach during his years at Milton High School. But the much larger Tate provided an opportunity to demonstrate he was an elite coach. Tate High School is a Pensacola-area school, specifically located in Gonzalez, less than fifteen miles from downtown. It is named for James Madison Tate, a local minister, attorney, and Civil War veteran who founded the school in 1878. It is set back from Highway 29, and an unobtrusive road sign points the way to the school from the highway.

Since its primary two-story brick building was built in 1917, Tate High School had grown from ninety-four students to over two thousand by the time Carl Madison became head football coach. The football team played in highest classification of Florida High Schools. In the days Madison served as its head coach, the football practice field was bordered by a pecan orchard that provided wonderful shade. Many a player stole a longing glance at the shady spot during three-to-four-hour practices under the hot Florida sun, but it was a treasure rarely enjoyed and might as well have been a mirage.

In 1971, many Tate High students were children of workers from the paper mill in Cantonment, and that is still the case today.

At the time, Tate principal Ralph Godwin said of bringing Carl Madison on board as the head football coach, "I feel we are very fortunate in getting a coach [with] the caliber of Madison. He's a very dedicated man and should be a tremendous help to our entire athletic program. His record as a coach is without question, and his dedication toward building young men is outstanding. I feel extremely lucky to have such a man build our athletic program."

At the time of his hiring, Madison said, "I'm happy to be getting back to the Pensacola area. My years at Forest Park have been great, but I have wanted to get back to Pensacola for some time. I have a lot of friends in Northwest Florida, and I feel Tate is a school on the move. I know jumping into a school which is in the Big Five Conference will be tough, but I feel it will be a great challenge."

Starting at Tate began the longest uninterrupted tenure at one school of Madison's coaching career. He inherited a once-proud Tate football program that had won the Northwest Florida Conference title as recently as 1967 but had not managed a winning season since. The year prior to his arrival, the Aggies posted a 1-8-1 record and were winless in twenty-nine of their previous thirty contests.

Tate wasn't alone in its struggles. Few of the local schools had achieved much success.

"When I went to Pensacola in 1971, football wasn't very good," Madison later said. In fact, none of the local teams had earned a spot in the state playoffs in recent memory.

Paul Bowers played for Madison's first Tate teams and later went on to incredible success in the business world, including eleven years as chairman, president, and CEO of Georgia Power.

He later stated what everyone felt when they heard Madison was going to be their football coach. "All of us who were players at the time heard about the coach, and all the rumors started. We heard the horror stories from Milton High School. That he was absolutely going to have blood coming out of our eyes. We were going to be running every day for hours and hours. And we were horrified."

Bowers went on to say that he and all his teammates were searching for something. They wanted an opportunity to be winners. They needed someone to push them. That person showed up in Carl Madison.

According to Bowers, "You learned the most from the losses because the next week was going to be so tough. He was asking you what did you not do and what are you going to change? What are you going to do to ensure your teammates are not disappointed the next time you're out on the field? He was searching for the soul of our team. When we walked out in uniform, who did we represent? Not only did we represent ourselves and our families, but we represented the others on the team. We represented a school. We represented a community that we went to school in. And he made sure we understood that. As I reflect back upon my career . . . it always comes back to how do you drive to be winners?"

Bowers was honored at a 2012 event in Atlanta for his support of education over the years. As part of the award, he was asked to recognize an influential teacher in his life. He chose Madison.

Carl and Grace [Madison's second wife] traveled to the event at the Fox Theater where Carl was recognized for his contribution and impact on Bowers' life. Nine years later, Bowers spoke at an event honoring Madison on the Coach's ninetieth birthday. Despite an incredibly busy schedule, Bowers would not pass up the opportunity to honor his former coach and communicate to those in the crowd the kind of positive influence one person can have on the future of many others.

Madison came to Tate in time for spring football practice. The difference between Madison and the Aggies' previous coach Manning Hitt was "like daylight and dark," according to Jerry Halfacre. "Manning was a real good guy, a good coach. But he wasn't that hard-nosed disciplinarian type guy. He was more of a fatherly figure."

Madison felt it was extremely important to get the community involved in the Tate football program, and one of the things he immediately did upon his arrival was to form the Quarterback Club. He needed a group to that would support the program and help provide the things he believed it needed to compete at a high level in Northwest Florida and beyond.

Heading into the jamboree that season Madison said, "We've got a long way to go here. We've got the athletes. It's just a matter of time before we can mold these athletes into a good football team." In another interview, he would be more open about the team's prospects. "I'm not crying or trying to hide anything, but it's just going to take time before we can compete with the good teams in the Big Five conference. If I thought we could win a certain game, I would tell you so, but right now we're lacking greatly in experience and size.

"This season we're going to be concerned for the most part with how our athletes progress. We've only got seven seniors on the entire club, so we feel like we'll be able to improve and build a good football team. Right now, we're trying to instill the proper mental approach in our kids, telling them they must have the desire to be the best. And with that desire comes the mental readiness to go out on and perform well on Friday night. Our goal is to win, but I'll know in my own mind if we're coming around, and that will be a sufficient measure of success for me."

On the same day that United States Supreme Court Justice Hugo Black resigned due to health concerns after thirty-three years of service, and scientists assigned an age of 4.15 billion years to the "Genesis Rock" picked up by astronauts from the moon on the Apollo 15 mission, Carl Madison made his debut as Tate's head coach. The Madison news was certainly less historic, but one would have a difficult time convincing people in the Tate community that was the case.

The Aggies opened against Big Five Conference foe, Woodham. The game has been overshadowed through the years by the infamous story of Madison getting caught spying on the Woodham practice the week of the matchup. It has been told by many people, and most considered it an urban legend.

In an interview for this book, Madison related what really happened. "I went to Woodham to scout them. I had driven my car and parked it by the railroad tracks, and they let the air out of the tires, but they didn't catch me. Anyway, all I know is the score was 7–0 [actually 10–7] in our favor."

Grace Madison, who was teaching at Tate at the time and would not marry Carl until 1975, heard the rumors about the incident and thought Tate should fire him if proven true.[4]

Jerry Halfacre—one of many Halfacres to play for Tate over the years—was a junior going into that season and would be the quarterback for Madison's first Aggie team. He accounted for all the Aggie points in the 10–7 victory with a rushing touchdown, the point after, and a field goal. Although an exciting start to the season, it proved to be the high point since Tate would face much tougher opponents the rest of the way.

The Aggies didn't taste victory again the rest of the year, losing all but the season finale against Escambia, which they tied 0–0. It was an inauspicious debut season for Carl Madison at Tate, and some doubt about whether he could turn things around likely arose among Aggie fans. But success at Ernest Ward, Milton, and Forest Park had demonstrated Madison's ability to change a program's fortunes relatively quickly. He believed he would eventually do the same at Tate.

When Carl Madison had come to Tate a year earlier, he attempted to persuade his old Atmore friend and former assistant coach Floyd Adams to join him by offering him the head basketball coaching position along with the ninth-grade football job. Adams was at Robertsdale High in Alabama at the time, and he turned Madison down in 1971. But

---

4   At the time Madison interviewed for this book, over thirty years later, he still hadn't told Grace the true story.

when Madison made the same offer a year later, he accepted. He served as the head basketball coach for a couple of years. In 1975, he became the varsity football offensive line coach and in 1977, the head baseball coach. He served in both of those capacities through the remainder of Madison's tenure at Tate.

Another extremely important addition joined the coaching staff in 1972. Before Madison came to Tate High School, he had never coached any black players. He began coaching against them while at Forest Park, but there were no black students at Ernest Ward or Milton while he was there and none who played football at Forest Park. When he arrived at Tate, there were just a handful of black players on the team, but they included two starters, Willie Gray and Joe Brown.

After his first year at the school, Madison made the decision to add Willie McCorvey to his staff. McCorvey was black, and Madison saw great potential in him. He was a recent Alabama A&M graduate and Atmore, Alabama native. Being fresh out of college, McCorvey was young and looked even younger. When Jerry Halfacre first saw him on campus, he thought he was a new Tate player and likely to take his quarterback job from him. McCorvey quickly established a fantastic bond with the players on the team, and they loved him. After six years at Tate, he went on to incredible success in football, with coaching jobs at Clemson, Alabama, Tennessee, and Mississippi State.

Going into the 1972 season, Madison's hopes were high for the Aggies. The school was now part of the Big Five Conference. Unfortunately, two key players, defensive tackle Steve Landry and safety Mark Conti, both suffered injuries prior to the season.

"If Landry and Conti hadn't gotten hurt, we could have a heckuva team," Madison said. He went on to say, "Our kids are going to have to learn to play while they're bruised up a little. A boy gets a little injury, and he thinks he's dying. He's got to get up and go."

Throughout his career, Carl Madison considered himself somewhat of an amateur physician, diagnosing injuries on the spot. He was often right, though no medical school ever chose to award him with an honorary degree. Broken collarbones, sprained ankles, pulled muscles, and various other injuries and ailments were all pronounced with authority by Madison. He witnessed a multitude of injuries over the years on the practice field or during games. Unless they were extremely serious, he expected you to pick yourself up and make your way back into the action. If not immediately, then certainly in a timely manner. Anyone who ever played for him would tell you that if you chose to lie down on the field for an extended time, you better require hospitalization. That was simply not something he tolerated.

Halfacre confidently thought that the 1972 season would be nothing like the 1-7-1 campaign of 1971. After all, the team only lost one defensive starter from the prior year. "We believed we were on the edge of turning it around. We practiced four or five hours every day. Where most teams practiced the kicking game a day or two before the game, we practiced every phase of the kicking game every day," Halfacre said.

Madison's Aggies opened the season against Woodham in 1972. Jerry Halfacre returned to the quarterback position with some experience at the position. Halfacre came up big, scoring a touchdown, and kicking two field goals, but it took a Mark Wilcox interception with 1:15 left to preserve a 19–12 Tate victory. Tate followed that with a 43–6 defeat of Tallahassee Godby, the one hundredth win of Madison's coaching career. With its second victory, Tate exceeded its win total from the entire 1971 season.

Defeats of Brewton, (AL) Neal, Washington, and defending Big Five champions, Panama City Rutherford came next before more than eighty-five hundred people who showed up to witness the Tate-Panama City Bay matchup at Tate. Both teams were unbeaten and tied atop the Big Five Conference along with Tallahassee Leon.

The contest proved controversial. The Bay coach called Madison before the start and told him his team was stuck in traffic and would make it to the stadium later than expected. He requested that the kickoff be pushed back from 8:00 to 8:30. Madison put up an argument but eventually gave in. He normally had the Aggies on the field thirty minutes prior to kickoff for warm up, so based on the situation with Bay, he instructed them to stay in the locker room a while longer. The Bay team got off the bus in full uniform just before 8:00 and demanded to play at the original 8:00 time as set by the contract. Bay had gone to Woodham and warmed up at their field. Madison was livid since his team was unable to properly warm up.

Bay took a 6–0 lead on a second quarter touchdown and held it until halftime.

According to Jerry Halfacre, Madison "was as angry as I've ever seen him. He tore the locker room up."

There can be no doubt that Madison was angry, but it is likely that he saw an opportunity to use that to motivate his squad. Madison told the team what had happened with the Bay coach, and a determined Tate football team took the field for the third quarter. The Aggies fought back early in the second half with a Roger Brown scoring run. When Jerry Halfacre added the extra point, Tate led 7–6. In the fourth quarter, David Talley ran for a touchdown, and Randy Boyd returned an interception for the final score as the Aggies won the battle of the unbeatens 21–6, and Madison secured one of his most satisfying victories.

The Aggies' luck ran out in a 17–16 loss to Choctawhatchee. A field goal by Halfacre, which was ruled no good, involved some disagreement among the officiating crew. According to Halfacre, the two officials underneath the goal post ruled the field goal good, but the head official overruled them.

Madison commented later, "We didn't play our best game at Choctaw. A couple of dropped passes and a crucial fumble along with a roughing the kicker penalty really hurt us. We can't afford to let down like that again this week or we'll be 6–2."

Later in the season, Tate was declared the victor via forfeit due to the Indians playing some ineligible players.

Pensacola High came next on the schedule, and the Aggies had never defeated the Tigers. The record in the series showed PHS with fourteen wins along with one tie. The Aggies dominated 39–0 and moved to the number thirteen ranking in the Florida Sportswriters' Association prep football poll for AAAA and AAA schools—the largest classifications.

The low point of the season came when the Aggies could not hold onto a fourth quarter lead and lost to Fort Walton Beach 24–14. The loss became even more painful when word came Choctawhatchee had upset Tallahassee Leon 8–7. Had Tate defeated the Vikings, a victory over a winless Escambia would have clinched a berth in the state playoffs.

With the possibility of the playoffs ended, Madison could not hide his dejection. "We felt all along Choctaw would beat Leon. We also knew what kind of football team Fort Walton Beach had, and we just didn't get ready for the game."

Madison's Aggies took out their frustrations on Escambia in the season finale, winning 61–6 to close out a 9–1 regular season with the Choctaw forfeit. They made tremendous strides from the 1971 season, and eight Tate players were named to the All-City team in recognition of their accomplishments. Halfacre was named the Player of the Year for Northwest Florida by the *Pensacola News Journal*, and Madison received Coach of the Year honors.

The Aggies played an outstanding Jacksonville Englewood team in the first Tate Invitation Bowl. Tate hoped to play in some type of bowl game, but since their playoff fate wasn't determined until the final week of the season, all the bowls were filled. So they created their own bowl and invited Englewood to come participate. It proved to be an exciting matchup and more competitive than many of the state playoff matchups that occurred around the state. After trailing 14–0 early and later 21–6, Tate rallied for a 21–21 tie with the final score coming on a Jerry Halfacre to Richard Conti pass.

Throughout his coaching days, Carl Madison looked for ways to improve, specifically with the offense. While coaching at Tate, he decided to go to Houston, Texas to see if he could pick up pointers on the veer offense that coach Bill Yeoman ran at the University of Houston. Yeoman played football at the United States Military Academy from 1946–48, where he was the starting center on the squad that featured

Doc Blanchard and Glenn Davis, the famed "Mr. Inside and Mr. Out-side," who both won Heisman Trophies during their times at West Point. Yeoman later spent eight years as an assistant coach at Michigan State before being named the head coach at Houston in 1962.

Of all the coaches who influenced Madison over the years, none did so to the extent of eventual College Football Hall of Famer Bill Yeo-man, simply because of the veer offense.[5] The veer required quick tackles, strong guards, and a center, along with a smart quarterback capable of making the correct decision about who carried the ball. It could be run out of a number of different formations and similar to the triple option in that it most often results in a running play. Madison's teams primarily ran the veer from 1973 until the end of his coaching days.

The 1973 Tate football team appeared poised for another strong season. The backfield included both Roger Brown and Gary Fleming. Randy Boyd was set to take over for Jerry Halfacre at the quarterback position. Three returning linebackers, Doug Riggan, Larry Touchstone, and Jerry Howell anchored the defense. Steve Landry, Ricky Hathaway, Mark Johnston, and Darrell Chavers manned the defensive line.

If there were doubts about how the team would react coming off its first successful season in a few years, an opening 54–16 win over Union Springs helped ease them. But things changed when they played Talla-hassee Godby. It took a final minute score for the Aggies to escape with a 15–14 victory.

Tate benefited from "scouting" of Godby. Jerry Halfacre, who grad-uated from Tate and was now a member of the Florida State football team, decided to stop by Godby to watch some of their practice since he knew they played the Aggies that week. One person asked him who he was, and he simply responded that he was on the Florida State squad—failing to mention any connection to Tate. As he left, he happened to see two familiar faces. Woodrow McCorvey and Neal Summerford, two of Tate's assistant coaches, had apparently been watching the entire time.

---

5   The veer offense draws upon multiple formations to confuse the opposition about
     who will be carrying the ball.

McCorvey wore his brother's Coca-Cola work shirt in hopes that he would not raise any suspicion.

The incident harkened back to Madison's "spying" on the Woodham practice during his first year at Tate and further demonstrated his willingness to go to extreme measures to gain any kind of advantage over his opponents. In the modern day, these types of things would be referred to as "gamesmanship." Those who were victims of such Madison subterfuge over the years would likely use different terminology in their descriptions of what took place.

The next game didn't require anything extraordinary as nine different Aggies scored touchdowns in a 75–0 drubbing of W.S. Neal. By this point, Scotti Madison was the primary quarterback. Scotti was Carl's nephew, the son of Carl's brother Charlie. He was an extremely talented athlete, one of the best Tate has ever produced. Scotti went on to star at Vanderbilt in both baseball and football before eventually spending time in the major leagues with the Cincinnati Reds, Kansas City Royals, and Detroit Tigers.

It was tough as a quarterback under Carl Madison. Being a family member didn't make it any easier. Jerry Halfacre recalls a time when Madison became frustrated with Scotti and told him, "You aren't good enough to be a Madison. I'm going to call you Smith."

Years later, Halfacre stated that if Scotti Madison walked into the room, he would call him "Smith," and Scotti would know exactly what he was talking about.

Despite the pressure of playing for his uncle, Scotti Madison ran for three scores and threw for three more in a victory over Washington that ran the Aggies record to 4–0. Panama City Rutherford came next and never challenged as Tate shut them out.

With Tate now established as a winner, people began to show up in droves. Before even entering the stadium, you could see the smoke rising from the grills at the concession stand and smell the hamburgers and hot dogs the closer you got. Dozens of each would be sold every Friday night but few during play because most people didn't want to miss any of the action on the field. It was best to grab yours before kickoff or wait in the long halftime line. But if you waited in line at the half, that meant missing the performance of the Tate band—The Showband of the South. More than a few people came just to see them. They were a two-hundred-plus member band who dazzled the crowd with their music and the precision of their marching. Over the years they would win multiple awards, including a Grand National Championship. They helped to create an incredible in-game atmosphere on Friday nights.

Tate pushed its record to 6–0 by defeating Panama City Bay before taking on Choctawhatchee who came in with a 5–1 record.

"We're expecting a sellout crowd to attend, and we don't think anyone's going to be bored by a lack of action," Carl Madison said.

Choctaw had beaten Tate three straight years going into 1973, and the Aggies were determined to end the streak. An estimated crowd of more than twelve thousand witnessed Tate put it away in the fourth quarter on their way to a 34–13 defeat of the Indians.

Tate's record stood at 7–0, and they ranked eighth in the Florida Class AAAA state poll. They added another victory in dominant fashion over Pensacola High School. The win, coupled with Tallahassee Leon's upset loss to Woodham, put the Aggies in first place in District 1-AAAA.

The Aggies then faced Ft. Walton Beach, who had ruined their playoff chances the year before. Tate faced a similar situation in 1973, beat the Vikings and advance to the playoffs. After leading 8–6 at the half, the Aggies fell behind 14–8. They ran their final play from their own twenty-nine-yard line. Madison threw a pass that was deflected but caught by Farron Simpson at his own forty. He raced down the sideline heading for a tying score but was caught at the one-yard line. With the loss, it seemed their playoff dreams had been crushed again.

However, word soon came that Choctaw and Leon tied 21–21, so Tate only needed to beat Escambia in their regular season finale to earn a playoff berth. Regarding the final play against Ft. Walton Beach, rumors circulated about how Farron Simpson could get so open, and years later,

Scotti Madison admitted that he ran in from the sideline.

This time Madison's Aggies took advantage of the opportunity given them. Ken Rollins scored two first half touchdowns on the way to a convincing win over Escambia. With the victory, Tate became the first Pensacola team to win a District 1-AAAA championship.

The Aggies faced Jacksonville Raines in the state playoffs, and it did not go well. Raines quarterback Terry LeCount, a future Florida State standout, threw for three scores and ran for another in a convincing 37–7 defeat of the Aggies.

Carl Madison shared his thoughts, "LeCount is a tremendous athlete and without him Raines would be an average high school football team. They were bigger than we were, but that has little to do with the outcome. We did not play well, but I know that Raines is not thirty points better than us."

CHAPTER FOUR

STALLED

WITH MADISON'S AGGIES now a proven winner, the community took note. Crowds at Pete Gindl stadium grew progressively larger each year. Steve Campbell, who later played for Madison at Tate and won national championships as a player (Troy State) and as a head football coach (Delta State and Mississippi Gulf Coast Community College), was eight years old in 1974 and still recalls his excitement about Tate football. On Friday afternoons, he could not wait for his father to get home from work. Upon his father's arrival, Steve would immediately begin asking to go to the stadium with kickoff still hours away. His idolization of Madison and Tate football, in general, consumed him.

"All I ever wanted to do was play at Tate for Coach Madison and win a state championship. I didn't think past high school," Campbell said.

Madison's 1974 Tate team took a step backwards. They opened the season with losses to Tallahassee Godby and Clearwater. Later, they suffered one of the worst losses of Madison's career: 34–0 to Gene Cox and his Tallahassee Leon squad featuring future Florida State stars Wally Woodham and Jimmy Jordan. The Aggies never managed to get on a significant roll during the season and finished 5–5.

Madison said, "I wish the season weren't over. It's a long way to September." Regarding his thoughts on the season just completed, Madison went on to say, "Inexperience hurt this year, too, [and] we didn't work as hard during the off-season. But I'll guarantee you we'll work hard this off-season. We're going to set our goal at winning the state championship, and I think that it is within reach."

One thing was certain, Madison would have his young men pay close attention to the little details as they prepared for a new season— and that wasn't limited to the football field. During one road trip, the team travelled to a restaurant and ordered tea. Upon receiving their tea, many of the players proceeded to add sugar and stir. Madison stood up and called for the team's attention whereupon he began to demonstrate to them how to stir their tea without disturbing the other patrons. There are likely sixty to seventy adults who stir their tea to this day the way Madison taught them.

Even coming off a 5–5 1974 campaign, the Aggies seemed poised to make a move. Scotti Madison was a senior and the offensive line had experience. As he mentioned at the end of the prior season, Madison felt Tate should at least be a contender for the district championship and could go even further.

The season got off to an exciting start with a 24–21 defeat of Panama City Mosley. Scotti Madison ran for 137 yards and scored two touchdowns, including the game winner with under four minutes remaining. After beating Mobile Blount, the Aggies prepared for a showdown with defending state champion and current number one ranked team, Tallahassee Leon.

The contest held special importance to Scotti Madison. He played dismally against the Lions the year before, going 0–12 passing while throwing two interceptions. Carl Madison was optimistic. "We feel like we can beat them . . . if we keep our heads up and don't have turnovers. We've got to block the stunts and move the football."

In 1974, the Leon defense had completely shut down the Tate offense. A significant reason was due to the play of Yancey Sutton, who spent most of the game in the Aggie backfield. He seemed to be there almost as quickly as Scotti Madison received the snap. Sutton was a great story, a deaf young man who would later go on to star at the University of Florida and even spend a brief period in the United States Football League (USFL).

During the summer before the 1975 season, both Scotti Madison and Yancey Sutton were invited to the University of Georgia for a recruiting visit, and they ended up roommates for the trip. During the visit, Sutton explained to Madison that he could read lips. This was a remarkable revelation and explained a lot about the prior year's game. The fact that Sutton could read lips meant he might have been able to tell the play call or the snap count. Modern day football viewers see coaches hold play sheets over their mouths so cameras or others can't see what they are saying. That wasn't an issue in 1970's high school football, but Sutton had an ability others didn't possess. When Scotti returned to Tate, he informed Carl Madison of his discovery. Madison said he would take care of things.

Leon entered on a seventeen-game win streak and unscored upon in 1975. It was close for a while, but Tate pulled away late to defeat the Lions 37–21. The offensive performance was an extreme departure from the year before, largely due to Yancey Sutton not spending the entire evening in the Tate offensive backfield. Carl Madison changed the snap counts in preparation for Sutton's lip-reading advantage, and Sutton received multiple penalties for jumping offsides. It was a historic victory for Tate, possibly their biggest to date.

Madison commented, "Certainly I would like to say it was just another game, but I can't because they were number one. I just feel that anytime we're prepared—the coaches as well as the players—we're going to win. The secret to winning or anything you do is believing in yourself and believing you can do it. This was the reason for our success against Leon."

Madison's comments echo back to earlier mentions regarding the importance of the mental aspect of the game. He believed his team could beat Leon, and that belief was instilled in his assistant coaches along with his players.

Tate's next contest came against Washington, and the Aggies started poorly. At halftime they trailed the winless Wildcats 7–6 but after some "encouragement" from Madison, the Aggies played much better in the second half and won 27–7.

Madison's team then struggled again against a tough Moss Point, Mississippi squad. The teams alternated scores the entire evening, but Tate found themselves trailing 28–27 with just over five minutes remaining. Starting on their own twenty-yard line, Scotti Madison drove his offense down the field and scored from a yard out to give Tate a 34–28 lead. The defense held on, and Tate ran their record to 5–0.

The Aggies then traveled to Clearwater and came away with a hard-fought 21–13 victory. They now ranked fourth in the state and faced a once-beaten Fort Walton Beach team with a 3–0 district record. The contest would almost certainly decide the district championship and who would advance to the state playoffs.

The matchup took place at Fort Walton Beach. When Tate trailed 21–12 in the fourth quarter, it looked as though the dream season was going to end. There were still games left to play, but making the playoffs seemed a virtual impossibility. But as long as time remained on the clock, there was a chance. They pulled within range on a seventy-six-yard drive capped off by a Mark Wass touchdown run, cutting the lead to 21–19. Following a defensive stop, the Aggies got the ball with time for one more drive. Starting on their own thirty-one-yard line, Scotti Madison led the Aggies down the field on a methodical 11-play drive. When he snuck the ball across the goal line with less than two minutes remaining, Tate led 26–21.

Once again, the defense stood strong when it needed to, and the Aggies walked off the field victorious.

An emotionally drained Carl Madison said afterwards, "This team never knows when it's beaten. We've been behind in just about every game this season, but these kids believe in themselves, and they just keep trying to score touchdowns and tackle people."

His team had inherited its personality from Madison. He didn't panic when things weren't going well, and neither did they. They stayed the course, did what they were instructed to do, and competed. The results spoke for themselves.

After the string of close contests, Tate needed a breather. They got it against Pensacola High School, winning handily 40–21. The next one against Escambia figured to be more of the same for the unbeaten and now third-ranked Aggies. But things did not turn out as planned. Escambia kicked a late field goal to defeat Tate 15–14.

"They deserve all the credit in the world—they played a magnificent game," Madison said of Escambia. "Our people thought they couldn't be beaten, and they just got it put to them."

He was going to make sure if his team suffered another loss, it would not be because of overconfidence.

Despite the disappointment of the loss, the Aggies still controlled their own destiny in regard to the district crown. A victory over Woodham would give them the title, and they took care of business, crushing the Titans 54–6.

The Aggies entered the playoffs facing a rematch with Tallahassee Leon. Madison felt the earlier contest with the Lions would have no bearing on this one. "Leon had an off game. We caught them flat," he said of the prior matchup.

The playoff matchup between Tate and Leon is still talked about by those who witnessed it. The Aggies scored first on a pass from Scotti Madison to Billy Smith. Leon answered with a Harvey Carruth one-yard run. Tate regained the lead 14–7 late in the first quarter when Madison ran twenty-eight yards for a score. Leon tied it at 14–14 on a Jimmy Jordan to Greg Everhart pass. Tate responded with a Randy Kittrell touchdown run before Leon tied it once again on what had to be one of the longest tackle-eligible plays in football history. Jordan completed the pass to Mozella Gainaus, who rambled ninety yards for the score, tying the score 21–21. The Aggies responded by driving down the field and scoring on Richard Water's two-yard run to take a 28–21 lead before both teams headed to the locker-room for halftime.

The defenses took over in the second half. Neither team scored in the third quarter. Midway through the fourth quarter, Tate drove into Leon territory but faced a fourth and twelve at the Lion forty-seven-yard line and chose to punt. The snap sailed over the head of punter Ronnie Stryker, and he was tackled at the Aggie twenty-five-yard line. Leon took only four plays to score from there and tied the score 28–28. It appeared the Lions would win in regulation when they marched inside the Tate five-yard line, but Jordan missed a field goal with 1:27 remaining. Things would have to be decided in overtime.

The rules for high school football overtime were different in 1975 than they are today. They played "penetration." Starting from the fifty-yard line, each team alternated plays, with the objective of moving as deep into the other team's territory as possible. After each team ran four plays, whichever side of the fifty-yard line the ball ended up determined the winner.

Tate got the ball first. Running back Mark Woss lost a yard on the initial play of overtime. On Leon's first play, Jordan hit Everhart for an eleven-yard gain to the Tate thirty-eight-yard line. The Aggies were in trouble already. On their second play, Scotti Madison threw an interception. Ironically, this helped Tate since the ball was now at the Aggie forty-seven-yard line. Harvey Carruth then carried the ball to the Tate forty-six-yard line, before Madison threw another incompletion. Carruth then dealt the Aggies a crushing blow, carrying the ball seventeen yards to the Tate twenty-eight-yard line.

Tate had one play left. Scotti Madison threw deep to Johnny Wells, but the pass was knocked down by Danny Unglaub. When Jimmy Jordan downed the ball on Leon's final play, it was over. The Lion's received one point for penetrating the farthest and escaped with a 29–28 victory, advancing them to the next round of the playoffs and ending Tate's season.

It was a bitterly disappointing end to a successful season but one that everyone involved with Tate football could be proud of.

"I wish we could play football twelve months out of the year," Madison said. "We're looking forward to our off-season program. We're losing some good players, but we have some good ones coming back."

In addition to those experienced returning players, Madison kept his eye on younger players from the junior varsity and freshmen squads who would eventually contribute to the team's efforts. Madison had a sense about kids who cared about football. A young Erik Hector, whose older brother Norbert Jr. played for the Aggies in the late 1970s and who later played a big role on the Tate teams of the early 1980s, recalled sneaking into the halftime locker room occasionally. He'd hear Madison screaming, putting together cuss words Hector had never heard before—at least not in a row. But Madison was always very kind to him.

Hector enjoyed taking pictures of the players. One Friday night Madison told him to put down his camera and carry his clipboard during the game. He said Hector should stay right by him the entire night. He got to do it for other games as well, and it was a tremendous thrill for him. Much like Steve Campbell, Hector idolized Tate football players before he was old enough to play.

Not many people outside the program knew what to expect from the 1976 Tate Aggies going into the season. Gone were key players such as Scotti Madison, Ronnie Stryker, Shawn Biggs, Roger Robertson, and Craig Fleming, among others.

"We haven't adapted as much as I hoped," Madison said before the season opener. "The season will depend a lot on that. I'm confident we can, but right now we're not smart football players."

One of his strengths as a coach was that he understood each team presented a different set of issues and he identified those issues early. With the 1976 squad, he knew that extra time would need to be spent improving their on-field decision making.

Despite the fact that his team might be inexperienced, he wasn't going into the season expecting lesser results. His nature wouldn't allow that. That nature didn't apply just to football. It was not a well-kept secret that Madison liked to gamble. In fact, he never attempted to hide it, and many knew that he enjoyed going to the dog track in Pensacola. He also made his way to New Orleans and their horse track on many occasions.

When casinos became commonplace in the southeast, he would frequent them, sometimes inviting coaches and friends to join him. He loved to play blackjack and would spend hours at the table. He also enjoyed gambling on college football and would occasionally bet on five or more games a weekend, though typically not the big ones. He might even wager on an Ivy League matchup. But he studied all the teams he bet on and felt confident enough to do so.

There is no telling how much he won or lost over the years. He couldn't tell you. But when he reflects on it, he figures that he probably lost more than he won. Yet he has no regrets regarding gambling. He enjoyed it, and it helped fuel his competitive nature.

The Aggies opened the 1976 campaign against Panama City Mosley with a 26–21 win prior to taking on Pine Forest. It was only the second year of existence for Pine Forest High School and their first season of competition in AAAA since their reclassification from AAA in 1975. The two schools would eventually play significant roles in the career of Carl Madison. The Aggies struggled but still managed to defeat the Eagles 17–7.

Following a loss to Tallahassee Leon, the Aggies beat Washington 36–0 before a tougher matchup against Milton. Johnny Wells raced sixty-six yards for an early touchdown, and Mike Sapp added another score, giving Tate a 13–0 lead at the half. It stayed that way until the fourth quarter when the Panthers added a score of their own, cutting the lead to 13–7. Mark Madison added a field goal with just over four minutes to play to stretch the lead. A last-minute touchdown and two-point conversion by Milton were not enough, and Tate held on 16–15. The victory pushed the Aggies record to 4–1.

After Mark Madison's field goal ultimately provided the winning points against Milton, *The Pensacola News* did a story about how important placekicking had become in the high school game. It featured Mark along with Woodham's Mickey Bentley.

Carl Madison spoke about the importance of confidence. "If the kicker has any doubt about his holder or center, then he's not ready to kick. The kicker has to blank everything else from his mind when he walks out to the huddle. He has to be thinking about nothing else but the ball."

Mark obviously was able to do just that in the important kick against Milton.

Tate came into their matchup with Pensacola High riding a four-year win streak against the Tigers and without a loss to them since Madison's first season at the helm. The streak continued with a 31–22 victory. Defeats of Ft. Walton Beach and Ocala Vanguard followed. The battle against Escambia would decide the district champion and a state playoff berth.

Madison expressed his thoughts about his 1976 Tate Aggies. "I've enjoyed coaching this team more than any other I've had. They're eager to learn, and all of them try as hard as they can. They don't have that much talent, and they're inexperienced and slow. But they're always working hard to improve themselves." Anyone who ever played for Madison would tell you that was about as much a compliment as you could hope for from him, and it would likely make them smile to hear it.

Five thousand fans showed up at Escambia's stadium to watch the showdown, and three minutes in, Escambia took a 7–0 lead. Touchdowns by Randy Kittrell and Mike Bennett later in the first quarter put Tate in front 12–7. Morgan scored again in the third quarter to give Escambia a 20–18 lead, but Bennett answered with a score to put Tate in front 24–20. With just over nine minutes remaining, Kittrell scored again. Nicknamed the Patriots after previously being called the Raiders and later the Gators, Escambia answered. They had one final opportunity to win, but the Aggie defense held on downs at their own twenty-three-yard line in the final minute to claim the district championship.

One regular season contest remained against Woodham. Although it had no bearing on their playoff opportunity, they still wanted to finish strong and did so in a 14–3 victory. Then their thoughts immediately turned to the playoffs and a matchup with top-ranked Tallahassee Godby.

"We're looking forward to playing Godby," Carl Madison said. "They're awfully quick and they're physically strong. But we'll put eleven men on the field just like they do."

Tate did put eleven men on the field; unfortunately, none of their eleven were Sammy Knight. Knight, the Godby quarterback, threw two touchdown passes, returned a punt for a score, and a kickoff forty-three yards in a 28–0 thrashing of the Aggies. The Aggies did not manage to enter Godby territory until the fourth quarter.

"We thought we'd be able to move the football. We didn't, and it surprised me," Madison commented.

For many years, Carl Madison passed out a sheet of paper to the incoming freshmen in his football program. Keith Leonard received one when he began at Tate in 1977. The following words are worth more than a one-time reading because they are just as true today and can certainly be applied to more than football. "The Tate Expectations" read as follows:

Pride: You are an Aggie. Act the part in and out of the public eye. Do not expect praise. We expect you to do your best.

Hustle: Emphasize hustling all the time. Alert people hustle.

Poise: Maintain a cool, methodical poised attitude whether you are excelling or not. Never show emotions to others. Never let your opponent know you are tired, hurt, or discouraged.

Physical Toughness: The basis of being an Aggie. Nobody can be successful without being tough. Do not let your opponent off easy. Never stay on the ground. Get after your opponent.

Mental Toughness: An intangible all great individuals and teams possess. Remember that one play does not make the game. One practice does not make the week, and one game does not make the season.

Forget what happened in the past and keep your overall objectives in mind. Do not let past mistakes or success affect your present or future performance.

Consistency: *You must rule yourselves, so you perform the same every day. We cannot succeed with people who occasionally give their best effort and the rest of the time they are loafing. Strive for consistency whether it is the first day or the last.*

Unselfishness: *Life is a team game. It takes more than one to play. Always think in terms of the success of the team and not in the success of yourself.*

*A **challenge** is not something you're sure you can do. An **opportunity** is a chance to do your best.*

These guidelines summarize what Madison expected from his players, not just at Tate, but everywhere he coached. They were nonnegotiable and not just suggestions on how to experience success as a high school football player. They were guidelines for life.

Over forty years later, Keith Leonard has them framed on his office wall.

Mike Bennett transferred from Woodham to Tate as a sophomore after a redrawing of the school boundaries with the addition of Pine Forest as a Pensacola-area high school. Bennett started the last three games of his freshman season at quarterback for the Titans and looked to be a future star, not only in football but in baseball. Madison was happy to have him.

In 1977, Bennett entered his senior year. At the time there were no formal summer workouts, and he wanted to ensure he would be in shape for the upcoming season but didn't know how to go about it.

"What did you do to get in football shape during your playing days, Coach, without all the modern workout equipment we have now?" Bennett asked Madison.

"I'd go out into the woods and run, pretending the trees were defenders while dodging them," Madison replied.

That is exactly what Bennett did that summer. Many years later he laughed about it while telling the story, unsure of whether or not Madison was pulling his leg.

Entering the 1977 season, Madison said, "We have the players to win it. This could be one of the best teams I've had."

Madison planned to run some wishbone formation in the upcoming season because of the stable of backs at his disposal.[6] Greg Gibbs, Harry Bailey, Mike Bell, Mike Bennett, McLendon Cook, Soloman Sutton, Ricky Werhan, Anthony Grant, and George Boren were all mentioned among those who could potentially carry the ball. Scott Watson and Rusty Towery expected to handle the quarterbacking duties.

"Offensively, we look strong—we're way ahead of our defense," Madison said.

The AAAA Florida high school Tate Aggies opened their 1977 season against a much smaller A classification Alabama school—the smallest classification—in Brewton, Alabama's Southern Normal High School. It wasn't one Madison wanted to schedule, but the alternative was no game at all.

"We couldn't find anyone else to play on that open date. We were lucky to find anybody to schedule," he explained.

Mike Bennett said later that the Aggies did not watch any film on Southern Normal, and at the time, most of the team did not know the location of Brewton, Alabama. As far as they knew, they were playing the best team in Alabama. Southern Normal wasn't the best team in Alabama or anything close. They'd played Pensacola Washington in 1972 and lost 87–0. They improved by two points in 1977 with Tate winning 87–2.

Madison commented, "We did not help ourselves by playing them. The game went pretty much as we had expected."

---

6   The wishbone formation is similar to the T formation but with the fullback closer to the quarterback and the two halfbacks further behind on either side of the full-back—thus shaped like a wishbone.

Tate beat Pensacola High 55–0 the next week and moved to number three in the state rankings before playing the number three team in Louisiana—Baton Rouge Istrouma. In that contest, a potential tying thirty-seven-yard field goal fell short on the final play, and Istrouma won 23–20.

Tate needed to regroup quickly since they faced an unbeaten Woodham team next in a crucial district matchup. The Titans had never defeated the Aggies, and they expected that to change.

Woodham running back James Bishop said, "Tate's not that good. They haven't played anybody except last week, [Istrouma] and they got beat. They killed a one A team and Pensacola High, but that doesn't mean anything."

In a tight battle, Tate looked as if it would fall short in the final minute when they trailed 13–10, but Danny Karp caught a desperation fourth-down pass for a twenty-six-yard gain to get the Aggies close. Then Ricky Werhan scored from one yard out with only twenty-two seconds remaining to give Tate a 16–13 victory.

Victories over Huntsville, Alabama Johnson High and Escambia preceded a tough matchup with an unbeaten Fort Walton Beach squad. The now third-ranked Aggies defeated the fifth-ranked Vikings on an overtime field goal by Madison's second son Sky, 16–13.

Tate suffered a bit of a letdown in an uninspiring 21–13 win against a 2–5 Washington team. An interesting event occurred during the Washington contest. During halftime, a snake appeared in the visiting Wildcat's locker room, causing the entire team and coaching staff to stumble over themselves as they attempted to exit.

Washington coach Sherman Robinson accused Madison of having the snake put in the locker room. Madison denied having anything to do with it and still does to this day. According to him, earlier in the day there was a snake on campus. Madison told a nearby student to get rid of it. The student chose to dispose of the snake in the girl's locker room. At that time, the girl's locker room also served as the locker room for visiting football teams. The snake apparently chose to stay hidden for most of the day, eventually deciding to make an appearance during halftime that evening, leading to a panicked mass exodus of all the Washington players and coaches.

Though he denied any responsibility for the snake incident, if you took a vote among local coaches of the day on which of their colleagues was most likely to place a snake in your locker room, Madison would likely be the landslide choice. The question is whether they would choose him because of some past questionable actions or to make themselves feel better about their own capabilities as coaches. There would likely be some in each camp.

Tate then faced Pine Forest with an opportunity to clinch the district championship. The Aggies fell behind 19–6 before putting up forty-nine straight points in a 55–19 victory. Once again, Madison's squad claimed the district title.

A final regular season matchup with Milton was for nothing but pride. Both teams had already clinched their district titles and playoff berths, Tate in 4A and Milton in the 3A ranks. The Aggies did not play particularly sharp, making some costly mistakes including fumbles and a few penalties, but they managed to escape with a 14–8 win.

A playoff date with Choctawhatchee came next.

Choctaw came into Pete Gindl stadium with a 10–0 record and the number one ranking in the state. Still, *Pensacola News Journal* writer Mike Globetti predicted a Tate victory. That prediction did not appear bold when word came that Choctaw head coach Eddie Feely—who later coached at Tate—had suspended three offensive starters, including quarterback Mike Blanchard.

As it turned out, Madison would probably have preferred they played. Blanchard's replacement, Mike Rodrigue, led the Indians to a 27–15 win over the Aggies. After falling behind 20–0 in the first quarter, Tate battled to within 20–15. Despite three excellent opportunities to take the lead, they could not convert.

During one of those opportunities, the Aggies ran a trick play, a fake field goal. Sky Madison, the kicker, pretended he had forgotten to bring the kicking tee onto the field and proceeded to run towards the sideline. As he ran off the field, the ball was snapped, and Sky turned and raced towards the endzone. It fooled the Choctaw defense, but Rodrigue, who also played defensive back, recognized the play in time to recover and bat the ball away before it reached Sky.

Steve Campbell, now eleven years old and whose older brother Gerald was a senior on the 1977 Aggie team, recalls crying after the loss to Choctaw. The only other time he can remember shedding tears over a loss occurred when Alabama lost the 1973 Sugar Bowl to Notre Dame 24–23. He believed that the Tate unit would be state champions and the realization that wasn't going to happen crushed him.

Madison blamed himself for some poor decisions. "We played a good game, but bad coaching and wrong plays called a number of times hurt us."

Though he could be an enigma, Madison's comments said much about his character. It was a heartbreaking defeat, and there is no question that some mistakes by players were costly, but he felt it important to bear the responsibility for the loss.

Tate had now reached the playoffs four times under Madison's watch but had yet to advance beyond the first round. With an emerging Pine Forest Eagles team prepared to make a run, two years would pass before another opportunity to change their playoff fortunes arose.

High school football seasons began in mid-September in Pensacola for many decades. In recent years, they've started in late August but no matter when the season commenced, players had to deal with extreme heat. Early season practices often came with temperatures in the nineties and high humidity. Madison took advantage of the Florida sunshine and often went shirtless while his players sweated through hours of practice wearing football equipment. The casual observer surely must have been bewildered to see a small, tan, shirtless man yelling and screaming at much bigger young men who followed all his orders to the letter.

While Carl Madison coached at Tate, he requested the shop teacher make a paddle for him, one with holes drilled in for better effect. When report cards came out, all the football players lined up to show them to their coach. Any grades below a "C" earned the player a lick from Madison's paddle. This went on for years.

Later, in the days before signals from the sideline, Madison would get together the players responsible for running in and out with the play calls. At Tate, they would gather in the weight room where Madison sat at one end and gave the player a particular play. That player then ran to the other end of the room to tell one of Madison's assistants the play. Any mistake earned a lick from the paddle. It certainly encouraged players to get the call correctly relayed in game situations, and no one ever questioned his approach in the manner. It simply wasn't done and did not occur to people that it might be an option. Most laughed it off, at least those who weren't subjected to it.

While Madison's methods might be frowned upon in the current day and age, it is certainly worth noting that he valued scholarship and accuracy. He knew that a very select few of his players would ever go on to make a living in the game of football, so the value of an education and following instructions would be critical to their future success. Of course, it would also help his teams win games in the present, and that part of the equation cannot be discounted.

Coming off the 9–1 regular season of 1977, the Aggies once again expected to compete for a championship, but many thought Pine Forest was the team to beat in District 1-AAAA given their returning starters.

Heading into the season, Madison said, "There will be more balance than ever before this year. I think we will have a good football team, but everyone else in the district is improved."

Tate opened the 1978 season by defeating Quincy Shanks 34–0 in a game that Norbert Hector and Tommy Bennett both blocked punts. A 27–0 win over an out-classed Pensacola High School squad followed.

Next came a matchup with Baton Rouge Istrouma, the only school that defeated Tate in the 1977 regular season. Istrouma came in ranked number six in Louisiana, and Madison expected another battle. "Always tough," he called them. The Aggies did not play well against the Indians in a 12–9 loss. Tate responded with victories over Woodham, Escambia, and Washington before taking on Lake City.

The contest with Lake City was one of the most remarkable and exciting of Carl Madison's coaching career. The first half was an offensive slugfest, and when the teams headed to the locker rooms, Lake City led 30–22. The Aggies scored twice in the third quarter, while Lake City added a score of their own. When the final quarter began, the teams were deadlocked 37–37. Quarterback Rusty Towery, who threw for three scores, broke free on a fifty-three-yard run, his second rushing touchdown, to give Tate a 43–37 lead, but the extra point failed. When Lake City scored and converted the extra point with two minutes remaining, Tate trailed. With twenty seconds remaining and the ball on the Lake City forty-seven-yard line, Madison called for a halfback pass. Towery pitched the ball to Dale Kittrell who spotted wide-receiver Steve Jinright open and lofted a perfect pass to him. Jinright raced into the end zone giving the Aggies an incredible 50–44 victory.

Then came Pine Forest with the district championship at stake. Days before, Pine Forest coach Roy Roberts expressed frustration with Carl Madison when Madison chose not to exchange films. "Coaches usually exchange game films of their last three games. Carl wouldn't give us his game films, and he fixed it where the other coaches had their films tied up so we couldn't borrow them either. We've scouted Tate and have our own reports on them. But the films are for the kids' benefit. This only fires our players up even more."

Madison replied, "We have plenty of film on them and didn't need any more. Plus they have scouted all our games."

He went on to accuse Roberts of switching their matchup against Niceville the week before from Tate's stadium to Escambia's field. The Eagles played their home games at Tate since they did not yet have a stadium of their own. Switching gave them an opportunity to familiarize themselves with the field where they would meet Tate.

"I bet he didn't tell you that did he?" Madison said to *Pensacola News Journal* sportswriter Robert Robinson. "Well, he'll be glad to know we're practicing at Escambia Thursday afternoon. . . . While he's out worrying about what I do, he'd better be out coaching trying to prepare for what might happen."

Robinson's interview with Madison occurred during a Tate practice and both sides shared concerns that spying might occur. During the interview, a suspicious car pulled up in the parking lot, and Madison sent someone to go check it out. The person returned and told the coach that it was "just two old ladies."

"Yeah, but you don't know who was in the back," Madison replied.

Six of the eight staff writers from the *Pensacola News Journal* picked Tate to win. A crowd of ten thousand showed up at Escambia to witness the battle. Things looked good early for the Aggies as Soloman Sutton broke free for a fifty-three-yard touchdown run on their second possession, giving Tate a 6–0 lead. The score remained that way until Eagles star running back Lebo Powell took a pass and raced fourteen yards into the end zone with just twenty seconds remaining in the first half. After the extra point, Pine Forest led 7–6.

With 8:13 left in the fourth quarter, Powell fumbled the ball while heading into the endzone, but his Eagle teammate Frank Jernigan recovered the ball for a touchdown and a 13–6 Pine Forest lead. The Aggies could not get closer than the Eagle forty-two-yard line the rest of the way, and Pine Forest held on for the district championship. It was the first loss by Tate to a Pensacola school since falling to Escambia 15–14 in 1975 and their fewest points scored since tallying only six in 1971 against Choctawhatchee.

The bitterness of the defeat obviously carried over into the Aggies' final regular season matchup when they lost to a much smaller Gulf Breeze team 21–20. Tate finished the 1978 season with a 7–3 record and no playoffs for the first time since 1974.

Norbert Hector Sr. was president of the Quarterback Club for a couple of years and had two boys play for Carl Madison at Tate, Norbert Jr. and Erik. They were both very talented and unlike so many parents of ballplayers, Norbert Sr. never wanted to interfere with their coach. He and Madison developed a mutual respect and then a friendship.

Regarding his tenure as president of the Quarterback Club, Hector Sr. commented, "We both understood what my role was. And that was to help him with his objectives."

They were never in conflict. At one point, Madison told him the football program really needed a new weight room.

Hector Sr. asked him, "Well how do we get it?"

Madison replied, "That's your job."

They ended up having a fundraiser selling blocks of bricks and raised all the money they needed—around forty-five thousand dollars—in just three weeks. When it came time for the actual construction, however, there was an issue regarding building permits. Madison had told Hector that wasn't needed on school property, but a building inspector told him that was wrong, and they did indeed need one. When Hector Sr. informed Madison of the problem, he was told it would be taken care of. Hector Sr. never heard anything about a permit again, and the weight room was built.

Dale Gilmore served as an assistant coach under Carl Madison and for many years was the head coach of the freshman squad. During one of those years, he approached Madison voicing concern that he had too many players—around eighty—and requested permission to cut some of them.

"Instead, take your fifteen best players and give them to Pete Wright on the Junior Varsity team," Madison said.

"Never mind," Gilmore replied, and he found a way to manage the large team.

Madison possessed a unique problem-solving ability.

Expectations for the 1979 season were not extremely high. Robert Robertson, Sports Editor for the *Pensacola News* predicted a 6–4 finish for the season. Unfortunately, Robertson's projection ultimately proved optimistic.

Madison's squad opened the season with overtime losses to Choctawhatchee and Huntsville, Alabama's Butler High. Another loss to Baton Rouge Istrouma put the Aggies' record at 0–3, the first time a Madison team ever began a season with three losses. It also ran their overall losing streak to five, dating back to the previous season.

Following the Istrouma game in Baton Rouge, while the team stayed in their hotel, some girls knocked on the door of the room occupied by Keith Leonard, Rocky Colburn, Robert Dortch, and Kenny Walraven. They came by to ask if the boys were coming to a pancake breakfast the next morning. Leonard invited them into the room.

Soon another knock was heard. Colburn looked out and saw Coach Madison. The boys panicked and told the girls to hide in the shower, but Madison did a search upon entering the room and found them. His players knew they were in big trouble. Although they went to New Orleans that night, they could not enjoy it because of the concern about the punishment they were going to receive. Sure enough, following practice the next Monday, the four stayed late for extra running. This went on every day after practice for the remainder of the season. To this day, Keith Leonard believes that Madison sent the girls to their room.

Tate finally got in the win column by defeating a previously unbeaten Woodham squad. "We had deserved to win before now. I'm glad the win came when it really counted," Madison said. He went on to speak of his team, "This was a team effort, and I'd like to single out Sam Bailey and Mark Davis on defense." Bailey had switched from quarterback to defensive end and Davis from defensive end to defensive tackle. "They were unselfish about the moves and have played well," Madison commented further. The move of Bailey to defensive end meant that the quarterback responsibilities now fell completely upon Keith Leonard.

The Aggies won their next four and with that came an opportunity to play for the district championship against Pine Forest. The Eagles came in with a 7–1 record and the number three ranking in the state. Madison said of the matchup, "We don't have any ability. But we do have class and tradition. But they have the talent." Pine Forest jumped on the Aggies early. Lebo Powell, Doug Houle, and Greg Hardin all scored first half touchdowns, and the Eagles led 19–0 at the half on their way to a

26–15 defeat of Tate and another district title.

Once again Madison's Aggies followed up a disappointing loss with a matchup against 3A opponent Gulf Breeze, with similar results. The Dolphins outscored Tate 36–26. For Madison, it meant the first nonwinning regular season at Tate since his initial one. The only solace for the team was an invitation to play in the Optimist Bowl against Crestview.

If some Tate players were disappointed at playing in a bowl game, Tommy Bennett wasn't one of them. He took the opening kickoff ninety-six yards for a score and added another touchdown on a twenty-two-yard run in the Aggies' 42–20 victory.

"I think I wanted to win this game probably more than anyone else to show the coaches we still had it in us to win," Bennett said.

After the 1979 season, it appeared Carl Madison's career might be at a crossroads. There was no question he was a good football coach who knew the game well, was intelligent, and got a lot out of his boys. But after eight years at Tate, he had yet to even win a playoff game. He fielded some very good teams but any who advanced to the playoffs were knocked out in the first round. The last two seasons Tate had not advanced to the playoffs at all. Maybe he was just one of a very large group, a pretty good coach but not a great one. Based on his record to date it was difficult to come to another conclusion.

CHAPTER FIVE

HEIGHTS AND DEPTHS

FROM THE OUTSIDE looking in, there was no reason to believe the 1980 Tate football team would be anything special given their performance the previous year. Carl Madison felt differently, though. In fact, he thought it might be the most talented team he'd had at Tate. The team included seniors such as Keith Leonard, Sam Brown, and Rocky Colburn—who would go on to play for Bear Bryant's final team at Alabama. There were a number of talented juniors as well including Erik Hector, who later signed with Florida State; Mark Sayers and David Miller, both of whom went on to play baseball in the Southeastern Conference.

Keith Leonard is now in his late fifties. Few people know Carl Madison as well as he does. As a child, he went to many Tate practices and games with his father, who worked at the school. Leonard recalls getting to play pickup basketball and flag football with the coach in those early days and witnessing his competitiveness.

The things Madison instilled impacted many of his players throughout the rest of their lives. Madison spent a lot of time during workouts talking to Keith Leonard about confidence and leadership. He didn't just want the quarterback to be a leader on the field, but off the field as well. He wanted Leonard to speak to people in the hallways who weren't part of the football program during the school day. Leonard still makes a point of speaking to everyone in the halls today in his role as Assistant Superintendent of Human Resources for the Escambia County School District. As Leonard began his senior year of football, he was the unquestioned leader of the offense and with that came pressure.

Paul Brown was also a senior that season. He recalled coming to Tate as a freshman and immediately being confronted by Carl Madison. Madison told him how good a ballplayer his older brother Joseph was and asked Paul if he was willing to do what it took to be great. Brown didn't know what to make of Madison, but he did all Madison asked of him. The year 1980 would end up being a record-setting one for him.

Things got off to a rough start for the Aggie team when Madison developed kidney problems shortly before the season started and spent a week in the hospital. When Tate played in the pre-season jamboree,[7] Floyd Adams, the offensive-line coach, took over the head coaching duties and while not showing much of the team's offense, lost 7–0 to Escambia in the team's first quarter but defeated Pine Forest 10–7 in the second quarter on a last second field goal by Carl Wehrspawn.

Tate opened the season against their old nemesis Choctaw. The Indians beat the Aggies in overtime in 1979, but revenge didn't factor into the equation for Madison. "You can't play with revenge on your mind, or you lose perspective of what you're trying to accomplish," he said.

Choctaw's coach Dwight Thomas said, "It's always a game not decided until the very end. The programs have immense pride and longevity. The coaching staffs are comparable, and the support of the communities in Gonzalez and Fort Walton is super. Football means an awfully lot to the people of Gonzalez and Okaloosa County."

Thomas went on to say, "We don't feel like Tate will have the home field advantage because we'll probably have as many people there as they will. And I can assure you we'll make as much noise."

The Indians had an outstanding running back in Arthur Humphrey,

---

7   A pre-season jamboree is essentially a series practice games to prepare teams for the upcoming regular season.

who went on to play at Ole Miss. Humphrey gained over one hundred yards against the Aggies in 1979 and he did so again that night, amassing 136 yards. Choctaw dominated throughout and led 19–0 going into the fourth quarter. Tate added a couple of touchdowns, one on the final play to make the final score a respectable 19–13, but still a loss.

Great coaches are able to accept responsibility when they fall short, and Madison never hesitated to point the finger at himself. He did so after the Choctaw game. Even though he was not at full strength, he said of the game, "I think my not being there [for practice] had a great deal to do with the loss. The team would have probably done better if I had not come back that week. We weren't ready mentally. The team expects the coach to be ready and when the coach isn't ready, you can't blame the team for failing," he said.

Keith Leonard on the other hand, blamed himself for the loss.

Even if he publicly accepted blame for the loss, he wasn't going to let his team off easy. The next week of practice was one none of the players on the team would ever forget. Frank Colburn Sr., father of Rocky, witnessed the practices and called them "the most brutal practices I've ever seen. The people crawled through the fence and went to the orchard and never showed up again, [one] transferred to Century."

Keith Leonard described the Monday practice as "the closest thing to all-out physical war that I've ever experienced."

One of the players, Joey Kite, required assistance to get to the showers that day. Leonard and Rocky Colburn were there to help him. "You're not going to die," they told him. Frank Colburn saw him, and he was not so sure. Kite did recover though and played great football that season.

The brutal practices paid off as the Aggies beat a Baton Rouge Istrouma team that had defeated them three years in a row in the second game of the season. Then Madison's bunch amassed 557 yards of offense in a 51–6 thrashing of Pensacola High. Randy Bonner caught three touchdown passes and all three Tate quarterbacks Keith Leonard, David Miller, and Jimmy McGhee, threw scoring strikes.

Tate faced Woodham in their district opener. "The season is just starting. It's not just another ballgame," Madison said. It was Madison's first matchup with new Titan coach Don Sharpe, who enjoyed tremendous success in Andalusia, Alabama as the head coach there. This one was no contest. Sam Brown scored four touchdowns while leading the Aggies to a 49–0 victory.

Roosevelt McNeil led the team in rushing with 127 yards against Woodham but left the team shortly thereafter. With other Aggie running backs banged up, Madison decided he needed options as the team prepared for Escambia. That week he had Paul Brown and Rocky Colburn practice at running back. Defensive coordinator Bobby Taylor didn't like the idea since the two safeties were so valuable to his defense, but once Madison made up his mind that was how it was. Taylor just requested that the two only be used at running back if the Aggies absolutely needed to score. During the contest, Madison inserted Paul Brown and called a running play.

Paul's first cousin Sam Brown, the Aggie fullback, told Paul, "just follow me."

Paul took the handoff, followed Sam through the hole in the defensive line, and proceeded to run sixty-six yards for a score. It was his only carry of the season. Randy Bonner added two touchdown receptions and Tate defeated Escambia 47–12, running their district record to 2–0 on the season.

A win over Fort Walton Beach preceded another one over Washington. As the 1980 calendar flipped to November, Tate looked strong and finally broke into the Florida Sports Writers Association top ten rankings at number nine. A matchup against a good Niceville squad offered a chance to climb even further. With two fourth quarter scores the Aggies pulled away for a 34–13 victory, and it was on to Pine Forest for an opportunity to win the district championship.

The Pine Forest Eagles had enjoyed tremendous football success in their short six-year existence. They won district titles the past two seasons, and each of those years advanced to the state championship game, losing to Merritt Island on both occasions. The 1980 Eagle team struggled, though. It came in with only a 3–5 record, but Pine Forest coach Roy Roberts felt his team would be up to the challenge.

"I feel good about this game," Roberts said. "I enjoy playing Tate. It's one game you don't have to get the kids up for because they get themselves up."

A crowd of over eight thousand fans showed up at Pine Forest's Lon Wise Stadium to see if the now seventh-ranked Tate Aggies could wrestle the district crown away from the Eagles. Tailback Marcus Sisco led Pine Forest to a first quarter touchdown that proved the only score of the first half as Tate trailed 7–0 going into the locker room. On the Aggies' first play from scrimmage in the second half, Sam Brown gained thirty-two yards. Brown carried the ball the next three times and scored on the third carry. When Wehrspawn added the extra point, the score was 7–7. It stayed tied until the fourth quarter when the Aggie offense drove eighty yards. Once again, Sam Brown scored and when Jace Banfell added the two-point conversion, Tate led 15–7. Later in the fourth quarter, Paul Brown recovered a fumbled punt on the Eagle forty-seven-yard line, and the Aggies drove the rest of the way with Brown adding a third touchdown in the final minute of play. By a score of 22–7, Tate claimed the district championship.

Madison recognized the importance of having talented players and that everything else being equal, the more talented team would almost always come out victorious. But he also knew how important good coaching was and that it could be—and often was—the difference in a contest.

He summed up his feelings after escaping with a win against the Eagles this time, "It's been two disappointing years. But Pine Forest had the better team those two years and still we had a chance to beat them. Tonight, I think we had the better team, of course it wound up that way, but Pine Forest had a good football team."

In the regular season finale against Gulf Breeze, nothing was at stake for the team other than staying fine-tuned and not suffering any injuries. One individual goal was still attainable though: in the history of

Tate High School football, no running back had ever gained a thousand yards rushing in a single season. Sam Brown came in 123 yards short of that milestone. He left with 6:32 remaining in the third quarter after breaking into the end zone for a touchdown. On the play, he hit 240 yards rushing for the night to finish with a total of 1,117 yards, while the Aggies rolled to a 49–12 victory, their ninth consecutive.

Shellie (Norton) Campbell was a junior cheerleader for the Tate 1980 football squad and later married Aggie player Steve Campbell. Shellie recalls that year well, how the school rallied around the team along with the excitement of the pep rallies and the games. A general confidence permeated everything. It was an atmosphere created almost entirely by Carl Madison. She always expected to win and was surprised when opposing teams even stayed close to her Aggies. As the team prepared for the playoffs, everyone hoped they would get to experience four more weeks of the incredible ride.

The 1980 playoffs began in Panama City against the number one ranked Mosley Dolphins. Before the game, the team was uncharacteristically nervous. Everything was quiet. Their rhythm was off. They were laying around in the locker room with nothing to do. They had a regimented schedule before every game, but it had been thrown off. Madison did something most had never seen him do before. He started telling jokes and made them laugh. It loosened them up. They were ready.

When they finally got out of the locker room to warm up, the Mosley teamed marched onto the field chanting in unison and pointing at the Tate players in an effort to intimidate the Aggies. Dolphin fans cheered, "Two-four-six-eight, we want Tate."

Madison turned to a reporter, winked, and said, "They're gonna get some of us too."

Mosley came in averaging three hundred yards rushing, and star running back Quinton Reed had amassed over seventeen hundred yards alone. They were without the services of their starting quarterback, John Little, who broke his collarbone the previous week. It was an incredibly hard-hitting contest, with most of the hitting delivered by the Aggies.

An argument can be made for sticking with what has worked for a team all season. But great coaches recognize when they need to venture away from what might be expected, especially when facing a team of equal, if not, superior talent. So for the first time all-season, Madison had his team come out running the wishbone. Carl Wehrspawn kicked a first-quarter field goal to put the Aggies up 3–0. Later, Mark Sayers caught a tackle-eligible pass from Leonard to give Tate a 10–0 halftime lead. In the third quarter, Jace Banfell picked up a fumble and ran sixteen yards for a score giving the Aggies a 17–0 lead. No more scoring occurred, and Tate knocked off the number one team in the state. The vaunted offensive attack of the Dolphins was held to a net gain of zero yards, and their star running back Reed gained only two yards. Tate running back Sam Brown ran for 150 yards.

"Our defense played an excellent game," Madison said. "I thought we could hold them to a touchdown and that we could score three touchdowns. We didn't quite get our three, but the defense shut them out, so I guess it came out about even."

His comments drove home that he was able to realistically assess his team and what they were capable of ahead of time. This was yet another area where he separated himself from most coaches.

Mosley head coach George Dean summed up the Tate effort. "They kept pressure on us all night long. Every time we would try to run, two of their secondary people were in our backfield. We should have gone to the pass earlier."

Some local reporters visited practice the next week, and while one of them surveyed the scene, a Tate player leaned over to say, "Hey, write something nice about the defense, okay?"

The reporter responded, "What's your name?"

"Erik Hector," the Tate player replied, grinning. "I'm a strong side defensive end. Don't forget now."

The article embarrassed Hector when it came out because he felt it made him appear as a braggart, when in truth he was extremely proud of his defensive teammates and just wanted some additional attention given to them as a unit. He spoke with Madison after it appeared, and his coach showed great compassion, giving him fatherly advice. He understood Hector's intentions no matter how others may have perceived them.

Tate faced Orange Park in the second round of the playoffs. The Raiders came in with a 9–2 record, but Leonard recalled later that after watching game films he expected his Aggies to win. Twelve hundred Tate fans made the long drive east on I–10 across the Florida panhandle and just south of Jacksonville. They expected great things from their squad, but some were awed in pregame warmups watching Raider quarterback/punter Ray Criswell, who would go on to kick at the University of Florida and for the Tampa Bay Buccaneers in the NFL, boom sixty- to seventy-yard punts consistently. Tate players were focused on the task at hand because they had been coached by Madison to do so. Besides, if Criswell got to punt a lot during the game, that would only be good news.

The Aggies scored on their first possession—a fifty-eight-yard drive capped by a pass from Leonard to Zel Brown. In the second quarter, Carl Wehrspawn kicked a twenty-one-yard field goal for a 10–0 lead. Later in the quarter, Rocky Colburn returned an Orange Park punt forty-six yards to put Tate inside their opponent's five-yard line. Three plays later, Leonard snuck in for a touchdown to stretch the lead to 16–0. With just under a minute to play in the half, Sam Brown broke loose for a twenty-eight-yard scoring run, and the Aggies went to the locker room with a 23–0 lead. During the halftime break, Frank Colburn Sr. overheard one Orange Park fan say to another, "These fellows [speaking of Tate players] ought to be wearing fatigues. They came for war."

Orange Park struck for two scores in thirty-one seconds to pull within 30–14 in the third quarter, but the Aggies did not panic. They settled down from there and won 50–14. If the defense was not quite as solid as it had been against Mosley, they still proved impressive, intercepting seven Raider passes, including three by Paul Brown. It was extra sweet for Brown after a Jacksonville reporter wrote earlier that Tate had not faced a passing attack like they would in the Raiders.

Madison said, "Our defense played a good game. Hell, we've just got a good defense. Nobody is going to throw on our defensive secondary." He continued, "I didn't think we'd score fifty points against them, but I did think we'd score five touchdowns."

Many Tate fans expressed frustration when they learned they would have to travel for the third straight week in the playoffs, this time to Winter Park, just north of Orlando and almost a seven-hour drive from Tate. For the players, it wasn't that big a concern. It would be nice to play in front of the home fans, but for a chance to secure a berth in the state championship game, they would go anywhere.

Grace Madison served as the cheerleader sponsor in 1980, and she decided to reward her girls for an incredible year with some fun on the trip. She would take the girls to Disney World for the day before their game that evening. The girls were excited and looking forward to the day, but as they left their hotel parking lot that morning, Grace backed into another vehicle, doing a fair amount of damage to her own car.

The accident upset Grace, but she wasn't going to let it stop their trip to Disney World. They made it and had a great time, but she insisted that none of them say anything about the accident to anyone until later. Just one victory from making it to the state championship, she did not want Carl distracted in any way from what he needed to do to prepare his team for such an important game. She'd deal with that when he won, because just like Shellie Campbell, she expected to win.

Winter Park had a good team—a very good team, in fact. Keith Leonard felt they were extremely similar to the Aggies. He believed his squad would win, but he did not have the same level of confidence as he did against Orange Park the week before.

Madison called Winter Park "a doggone good football team. Their defense is the probably the best we've seen in the playoffs, and their offense is the big play type."

Winter Park did not have the same atmosphere that Tate had been accustomed to throughout the season. They had loyal fans, but perhaps due to being close to Orlando and all that came with a big city and the things it had to offer, including Disney World, their passion for the local team didn't appear to match Tate's. Still, the Wildcats came in unbeaten and a confident bunch. Their fans shared that confidence, proclaiming loudly enough for some Aggie fans to hear in the stands that no one could stop their option attack. They were about to find out differently.

Tate jumped out early on a field goal by Wehrspawn. In the second quarter, Sam Brown broke loose for a fifteen-yard touchdown run, which made the score 10–0. It stayed that way until halftime. With less than five minutes remaining in the third quarter, Brown added another score, and the Aggies grabbed control 17–0. Winter Park had an opportunity to get back in the game early in the fourth quarter when they drove inside the Tate five-yard line. On fourth and goal, Paul Brown tipped a pass, and when Kenny Walraven caught it for the interception, it was all but over. Tate held on the rest of the way and with that came a date for a state championship.

When asked if any one player's performance stood out, defensive coordinator Bobby Taylor said, "We thought if we stopped the tailback and the quarterback from running with the ball, we'd have a very good chance of winning. We did that, and it was a team effort. You can't really cite any one player because when you get this far, everyone played a key role."

Madison had been angered earlier in the day when he read comments by Winter Park coach Larry Gergley asserting that Tate often resorted to trick plays to defeat their opponents. The comments were not well considered. It had been proven numerous times over the years that you didn't want to offend Madison. He was a proud man and was proud of his players, too, defending them regularly. The 1980 Tate squad was the last one you'd want to give any additional incentive.

Madison responded to the perceived slight after the game by saying, "Our trick plays were to knock their tails off every chance we got, and we got plenty of chances."

Tate's opponent in the state championship game was Miami Christopher Columbus. The week leading up involved controversy on where the contest would take place. Columbus had played all three of its playoff games in the Miami area, while Tate had not played anywhere close to home, traveling a total of nineteen hundred miles the previous three weeks. It originally appeared that Miami was willing to travel to Tate to play, but Columbus principal, Brother Edmund Sheehan, balked on that idea after giving it more thought. According to the bylaws of the Florida High School Activities Association, if two teams met in a state championship game and the distance between the two schools was greater than five hundred miles, then either principal could request a neutral site. On Monday of championship week, it looked like Tallahassee's Capital Stadium was where it would take place.

As things turned out, Tate did not get to play at their home stadium, but they got the next best thing, Pensacola Escambia's stadium. After the FHSAA committee upheld a ruling for it to be held in Tallahassee, Fred Rozelle, secretary of the committee, placed a call to Columbus Principal Sheehan, to ask if he would reconsider playing at Tate. Sheehan insisted that he did not want to play at Tate but would play in Pensacola. Tate Principal Ralph Godwin then secured Escambia's stadium.

"We appreciate what Columbus has done," Godwin stated. "They could have continued to insist that the game not be played here. They believe Tate would have a bigger advantage on its home field, so they asked that we play at another stadium. We are so happy to get the game in Pensacola that we aren't going to argue about the stadium."

Carl Madison was relieved. "We finally know where we're going to play . . . now we won't have to keep answering the phone. I don't think the players were affected by not knowing where the game was going to be played. I don't believe they thought a whole lot about it."

Both teams came in with 12–1 records. Each of their losses came early in the season—Tate's 19–13 to Choctawhatchee in their season opener, and Columbus' 38–6 to Miami Killian in their second contest.

Some thought that Columbus might just be a team of destiny. In their first playoff game, they trailed South Miami 20–14 with less than a minute to play. The Cobras only needed to run out the clock, but they fumbled, and Explorer defender John Bass picked up the ball and ran it in for the touchdown giving Columbus a miracle 21–20 victory.

The five writers for the *Pensacola News Journal*, and guest picker PJ Smith, did not subscribe to any "team of destiny" nonsense and all picked Tate to win. They had seen enough of the Aggies to convince them that they were not going to be denied a state championship.

It was Madison's second opportunity at a state championship, the first coming at Forest Park, Georgia when his team lost to Valdosta. "I really can't say this is just another game because it isn't," Madison stated. "But my feelings are we've got to get ready for this doggone game, so there's no need to get nervous and all uptight. All the travel we've done the last few weeks, the controversy as to where the game would be played, and just trying to get ready to play all has helped to take it off my mind."

Madison may not have been nervous, but his assistants were and they were not afraid to admit it. Bobby Taylor said, "I'll have to admit I have gotten a little bit nervous. I think the closer you get the more nervous you get. Big games like this usually don't bother me until the night of the game. But the kids seem relaxed and loose, and that's the big thing."

Taylor did not consider himself superstitious but admitted to wearing the same pants, shirt, sweater, and shoes for the previous five contests.

Players had different reactions to the pressure. Erik Hector broke out in hives during the week. Sam Brown admitted to not being able to focus on schoolwork.

Offensive lineman, Tommy Wright, when asked about all the excitement responded, "What excitement? It hasn't hit me yet. We've been so involved in trying to get ready for the game. I guess it'll hit me Saturday morning."

The morning of the championship, the head of the English department at Tate, Wilhelmena Boykin, brought a bell to school and showed it to Keith Leonard. She told him she had rung the bell exactly twenty-two years ago to the day, when her son played in the Illinois state championship and won, and that she'd have it that night.

"When she told me that story, I knew there was no way we were going to lose. It was too good of an omen for it not to work," Leonard said.

The game was a sellout and broadcast live on television. The stands were filled primarily with people wearing red and pulling for the Aggies, but a good contingent of Columbus supporters made the long journey to Pensacola and were loud in support of their Explorers. Some held signs that read "Beat Pensacola," which seemed odd to Tate fans since no one ever referred to them that way. They were Gonzalez Tate. Still, the Aggies walked onto the field with the opportunity to do something no other Pensacola-area team had ever done, win the large school state championship in the state of Florida.

Both teams seemed to come out tight, and the first quarter was a defensive struggle. Eventually, Tate managed to drive inside Columbus territory on one occasion where they faced fourth and one yard at the Explorer forty-nine-yard line. Madison intended to go for the first down, but when the Aggies drew a penalty, he chose to punt. The quarter ended 0–0.

In the second quarter, Tate finally mounted some offense. Following an eleven-yard punt by the Columbus punter, the Aggies took over on the Explorer thirty-eight-yard line. Five plays later, Keith Leonard ran it into the endzone from thirteen yards out, and Tate led 7–0. The Explorers responded with an impressive eighty-yard drive that culminated in a touchdown pass from quarterback James Desmond to John Adams. The teams went into their locker rooms at halftime tied 7–7.

Madison was calm at the half, which surprised many. He told the players they had twenty-four minutes left, and it was up to them whether they would be state champions. Madison had a trick up his sleeve though. He planned to come out in the second half running out of an entirely different formation, the *T*. Just as his unexpected move to the wishbone had worked against Panama City Mosely, this one would pay dividends.

On the opening play of the second half, the Aggie players, coaches, and fans experienced a tremendous change in emotions. Tate halfback Doug Lee broke loose on a twenty-seven-yard run but fumbled at the end of the run, and Columbus took over on their own forty-one-yard line. The Aggie defense needed to take charge, and they did. The Explorers ran three plays before being forced to punt. Tate took over on their own twenty-six-yard line and started their biggest drive of the year. Nine plays later, Ronnie Smith ran in from sixteen yards out, and Tate led 14–7. The Aggies forced Columbus to punt again on their next possession, and this time Leonard led his team on an eight-play, sixty-six-yard drive capped by Sam Brown's one-yard scoring plunge. With 2:48 left in the third quarter, Tate's lead was 21–7, and things looked good for the Aggie faithful.

Early in the fourth quarter, Tate mounted another drive that appeared to be stopped when Leonard fumbled, and Columbus recovered. The Explorers received a facemask penalty on the play though, and the Aggies maintained possession. Ronnie Smith added his second touchdown a few plays later, and Tate led 28–7. Midway through the quarter, defensive back Paul Brown, who had already set the state record for most interceptions in a season, intercepted a Desmond pass and returned it fifty-three-yards for an apparent touchdown, but he received an unsportsmanlike conduct penalty when he raised the ball in the air and high stepped on the way to the endzone.

Brown would later say that it was just a heat of the moment thing, and as he ran the ball back, he thought to himself, "What the heck?" and held the ball up in the air.

The fifteen-yard penalty gave Tate the ball on the Columbus twenty-one-yard line. They drove the rest of the way, and backup quarterback David Miller hit Paul's brother Zel on a three-yard jump pass for a score. Paul and Zel decided they would tell people they planned it that way all along. Wehrspawn added the extra point to make the score 35–7. It ended that way, and the Tate Aggies were state champions.

Fans stormed onto the field, many offering Madison and the others their congratulations. Some picked up Sam Brown and carried him on their shoulders. People that had watched Tate football for thirty years or more, along with small children, joined the celebration.

"Well, we finally did it, didn't we? We finally brought a 4A state championship to Escambia County. I'd have to say we did it rather convincingly, too," Madison said in the aftermath. "This probably is the finest group of young men I've ever been associated with in my ten years at Tate. They truly are a bunch of fine, young, Christian men. I think that character and strength came forth for us tonight in these young men. It'll be something they carry with them for the rest of their lives."

After he had finally reached the pinnacle, winning what had proved to be so elusive throughout his career to this point, he chose to speak of his players' character and strength and how important that would ultimately be.

A week later, Madison reflected on the Aggie squad. "They were a great football team. We really had a good team in all phases: good running backs, good receivers, good quarterbacks, good linemen, good linebackers, good defensive backs — we were almost a complete team."

Carl's wife Grace loved the 1980 team, not because of the state championship, but because of the boys. "They were just the best group of kids." She never experienced any trouble with them and at one point called Keith Leonard's father Dwight to tell him how proud she was of him for something he had done to help another student out. It was a special group of young men that accomplished great things, not only for Tate High School but for Pensacola area football.

Carl Madison pushed his players hard everywhere he coached. He believed they were capable of accomplishing things they might not believe was possible. So, he often pushed them to the very edge. He wasn't overly sentimental or perhaps sentimental at all. But he could show compassion, and he often did things out of kindness. During his Tate tenure, on a particularly hot Florida afternoon, he had a pickup truck full of watermelons parked under the pecan trees just off the practice field. When his young men completed practice, they all got to enjoy the watermelons as their coach looked on. He was proud of how hard they had worked, and it made him happy to see them enjoying themselves. Former players still recall that day. Madison had a way of creating memories.

In 1981, for the first time in the school's history, Tate High took the field as defending state champions. Although the team lost numerous talented players to graduation, they had enough talent returning that the Florida football writers selected them the number one team in the state headed into the season.

Going into the season, Madison said, "We'll probably have to pass the ball more this year because we just don't have the size we need to block for the run. We're so young. But we're getting to do things better. It's just a matter of time. I just hope the boys have pride to keep in there battling."

Unfortunately, the projected starting quarterback, Jimmy McGhee, suffered a broken jaw and could not play early in the season. David Miller, set to be a wide receiver that year, stepped in for McGhee until he could return from his injury.

The offense struggled in the season opener against Butler High School of Huntsville, Alabama. Although David Miller scored two touchdowns, he also threw four interceptions. Fortunately, the defense performed well. Tim Thomas intercepted two passes, and Steve Campbell, who after years of watching Tate football, played in his first varsity game, recovered a fumble for a touchdown and added another fumble recovery. When the final whistle blew, Tate had an ugly but convincing 27–7 victory.

Next on the schedule came Choctaw, the only team to defeat the Aggies in their 1980 state championship season. Tate had won fourteen straight since that defeat and avenging the loss of the previous year was on the minds of some. Madison continued to praise his defense in the week leading up to the contest but wasn't as comfortable with the progress of his offense. The matchup with the Indians demonstrated why he felt the way he did. In a defensive struggle, aided by poor offense on both sides, Tate fell once again to the Indians by a score of 7–0.

A Pensacola High team that had suffered twenty-one straight defeats was just what the doctor ordered to get the Aggies back on track, and they ran away 47–0. Next came a key district matchup against a much-improved Woodham team. The Titans lost to Tate 49–0 the prior year, but their coach Don Sharpe wasn't accustomed to losing and had already turned the program around. The question heading into 1981 was whether it had reached the level of Tate.

Sharpe and Madison were both incredibly competitive and obviously wanted to gain the upper hand over the other. Sharpe said of Madison in the week leading up to their meeting, "He is very well respected by everybody, and he deserves that respect because of the success he's had here. I feel like when you move, like I did, nothing follows you. You start all over. So, here I am a new kid on the block just trying to get established."

By the time it ended, Sharpe was established in Pensacola.

Three first-quarter fumbles by the Aggies cost them dearly, one of which was returned ninety yards for a touchdown and another which led quickly to a second score. Tate trailed 14–0 at the end of the first quarter. A McGhee touchdown pass to Zane Price narrowed the deficit to 14–7 just before the half, and it looked like the Aggies might have gotten it together. The third quarter saw one of the more impressive drives in Florida high school football history when Woodham took the opening kick-off and proceeded to go on a twenty play, eighty-two-yard scoring drive that ate up all but twenty-five seconds of the quarter. Tate added a fourth quarter touchdown run by Doug Allen, but that wasn't enough for the Aggies and Woodham won 21–14.

A dejected Madison commented, "They deserved to win. We weren't ready. A championship team doesn't make the mistakes we made." Again, Madison did not place the blame solely on his players. The collective "we" included himself and his coaching staff. Sharpe declared it a program-changing victory for the Titans, and it certainly proved to be.

Days later, Madison stated, "We've lost before, and we're going to lose again. What we have to do now is win our next two games against

Escambia and Pine Forest and hope that one of them can beat Woodham if we hope to win the district." Tate got the opportunity to handle part of that scenario the next week against Escambia and rolled 32–0. Victories over New Orleans Walker and Fort Walton Beach followed. Then Tate took a trip to Tallahassee to take on Leon High, led by their legendary coach Gene Cox. It had been a while since the two-schools squared off, and this night was reminiscent of some of their earlier matchups. In a contest that saw two Tate running backs, Doug Allen and Ronnie Smith, rush for over one hundred yards, the Aggies could not match the scoring of Leon as the Lions won 47–31.

Tate faced Pine Forest in the season finale. The past few years the matchup decided the district championship, but it was just for pride on this occasion since Woodham had already clinched the title. Still, it was an exciting high school football contest. A Jace Banfell field goal in the final minutes sent it into overtime, and the Aggies went on to win 30–24 in two overtimes.

With only a nine-game schedule in 1981, Tate accepted a bid to play in Citronelle, Alabama's Oil Bowl against West Jefferson High of New Orleans. "They called us and asked if we were interested in it, and of course, we were," Madison stated. He went on to say, "I'm sure our players wanted to play. In fact, if we could find another one, we could play again next week because in Florida you can play eleven games."

West Jefferson had a strong team that suffered only two losses during their season, one of them to the eventual Louisiana state champions. They also featured a star running back in Garry James who went on to gain over two thousand yards at Louisiana State University (LSU) before spending three years in the NFL with the Detroit Lions. Things did not look promising at the half when West Jefferson took a 14–0 lead into the locker room, but the Aggies put together a strong second stanza to win 23–20.

It provided a positive finish to a season that might otherwise seem disappointing coming a year after winning the state championship. Still, Tate had built a strong tradition of success at the highest level of Florida high school football, and it would be difficult to suspect that would not continue in 1982. But plenty of drama and change was ahead in the coming months.

Tate opened the 1982 season against Huntsville Lee at home and managed to escape with a 22–20 victory when Lee missed a field goal on the final play. The next week saw a matchup with the Choctaw Indians, a thorn in the side of Tate for a few years now.

Choctaw coach Dwight Thomas said, "It's time for a great football game that occurs between the Aggies and the Indians. It's a game of tradition, pride, and two great bands, the spirit, the fans . . . it's just a great rivalry." Thomas went on to discuss the lack of experience for both teams.

Madison said in response, "It will be a typical game regardless of whether the teams have no experience or a lot of experience. We'll play it tough, and I expect it to be a pretty low scoring ballgame." Madison proved prophetic.

"If you don't believe in miracles, you should have been at Gonzalez Tate High Friday night to see the Aggies pull a 13–12 win right out of the hat against rival Choctawhatchee," began the story from Ken Jordan of the *Pensacola News Journal*.

Trailing 12–6 late, they began a drive on their own three-yard line. After securing a few first downs, the big play came on a Randy Burns pass to Steve Campbell, who caught the ball at the Choctaw eleven-yard line and danced his way to the one. Burns snuck the ball in from there with less than a minute to play, and Tate escaped 13–12.

"We showed a lot of poise," Madison commented. "We knew we could come back. If we're within a touchdown of a game, we can usually win it."

A blowout defeat of Selma Keith ran the Aggies record to 3–0 before they faced their most important matchup of the year against Woodham.

Madison downplayed his team's chances. "They have to be two or three touchdown favorites. They're bigger and faster than we are. Legitimately, they have eight college prospects. There's no telling just how good they are. If we play well, it will be a low-scoring contest. If we don't play well, it will be a high-scoring contest for Woodham."

Madison was accurate in his assessment of Woodham. The Titans coasted 28–0 in front of fourteen thousand fans at Pete Gindl Stadium.

Tate then took a trip to Mississippi to take on Biloxi High School. The Aggies did not respond well at all from the loss to Woodham as they struggled mightily on offense and fell to the Indians 11–6. A defeat of Escambia moved their record to 4–2, and despite the loss to Woodham, they appeared headed for another successful season.

Losses to New Orleans Walker High School and Fort Walton Beach dropped the Aggies' record to 4–4 ahead of a matchup with Talla-hassee Leon. Carl Madison and Gene Cox of Tallahassee Leon enjoyed a competitive, yet friendly rivalry during their years coaching against one another. By the time they retired, they were the two winningest football coaches in Florida High School history with Cox first and Madison second. Later, in 1985 when Cox was selected the head coach of the first Florida-Georgia All-Star Classic, he chose Madison as his running backs coach.

In 1982 however, the rivalry remained on the competitive side. Cox later related that whenever his Leon team travelled to Tate, the phones that allowed his coaches in the press box to communicate with those on the field seemed to mysteriously quit working at some point. Cox also stated that whenever his teams travelled to Tate, they made sure to bring their own toilet paper. He did not put anything past Madison to try to gain an edge.

Cox decided the contract needed to state that the phones must be in working order. It proved a wise move on his part since the phones were not in working order that night when it came time for kickoff. Cox pulled out the contract and showed it to the officials. The phones mirac-ulously worked shortly thereafter.

The contest with Leon was the final home one of the season for Tate, and the Lions came in unbeaten. It proved to be a wild one. Aggie star running back Doug Allen, who went on to play for Alabama, rushed for 227 yards, which on most evenings would have been what everyone remembered. Unfortunately, his Lion counterpart at running back, Darren Holliman, ran for 432 yards as Leon prevailed 50–21. With time winding down, Cox called time out to give Holliman one more carry and a shot at the state record for rushing yards in a game. Holliman proceeded to run forty-nine yards for a score on the final play.

The losses took a toll on everyone from the coaches to the players and the fans. It was not what those associated with the Tate program under Madison were accustomed to.

Steve Campbell would later say, "I remember games feeling like my group was disappointing Coach Madison. I remember being embarrassed and ashamed that we had on Tate jerseys. Coach Madison deserved better than we were giving him."

Though Campbell felt the ties to Tate football stronger than just about anyone, his statement expresses how, although Madison was tough on his players—incredibly so at times—most had great respect for him.

Only a date with Pine Forest remained on the schedule. With it came an opportunity to end a four-game losing streak and finish the season with a .500 record. It was not to be. The Eagles prevailed 21–13. Though no one knew it then, Carl Madison exited the field as Tate head coach for the final time. Eventually, he would return to the Pine Forest stadium on the other sideline and add even greater glory to his illustrious career.

There is much controversy over exactly how and why Carl Madison's coaching tenure at Tate ended. It essentially came down to a select few powerful Tate boosters forcing the hand of principal Ralph Godwin for reasons other than just performance on the field. Although Godwin previously assured Madison he would return as the coach, things changed early in 1983.

In a meeting with Madison, Godwin told him he would not return as the head coach.

"Well, I'm not resigning," Madison said to Godwin. Following some back-and-forth, Madison eventually agreed he would resign.

On January 18, 1983, Carl Madison submitted a powerful letter to

Ralph Godwin, Tate High School Principal. The *Pensacola News Journal* published it the next day.

> *Dear Mr. Godwin:*
>
> *Please accept this letter as my resignation with protest as athletic director and head football coach at Tate High School effective June 30, 1983.*
>
> *My reasons for protesting are many, including the following:*
>
> *I have done an excellent job as head coach and athletic director during my tenure at Tate High School as measured not only by scores, numbers, and championships, but also by the multitude of young athletes who have entered my tutelage and left with improved bodies and more confident minds.*
>
> *Coaching to me is more than a job, more than a career, even more than a profession; it is my life. I love sports, and I love coaching. This is the most challenging and fulfilling aspect of my life. While at Tate High School, with the help of many fine coaches, the faculty and others, I have brought the spirit and fame of Gonzalez Tate to unprecedented heights to the envy of the competition. In short, I love coaching, and I am good at it.*
>
> *None of us is without faults. If each of us were measured by his faults alone, certainly we would all fail. When tested against what others expect and demand of us, there are no perfect scores. What really matters to a man is how he honestly measures himself against what is expected of him by his Maker as he understands Him, and how he achieves the goals to which he himself aspires. In my case, it is noticeable that public tolerance of my perceived faults is inversely proportional to the win-loss record of the football team.*
>
> *As social animals, most of us seek acceptance and companionship from those around. I have striven to be a responsible citizen and a credit to the community. Largely, I feel that I have succeeded.*

Sincerely,

Carl Madison

Madison's longtime friend and colleague Floyd Adams later said, "It was unbelievable really, that they would do that to him with what he had done for that school and community. And not only that school but for football in Northwest Florida. Carl set the standard by which every other ballclub . . . in the Panhandle area tried to measure their team as to how they could be competitive. It was the biggest mistake Tate High School ever made, letting Carl go."

Madison's son Sky said later, "It was tough for a long time [to root for Tate]; still a lot of bitterness. That was a pretty hard time for a lot of people. He *was* Tate. Ever since then, Tate hasn't been the same."

Almost forty years after Carl Madison's departure from Tate, Sky's statement still rings true.

Almost a decade later in January of 1991, Tim Thomas, who played defensive back under Madison on his final Tate squad, was serving as a first lieutenant in the Army with the 1st Calvary Division in Saudi Arabia during Operation Desert Storm. Below are excerpts from a letter he wrote to his parents that were later published in the *Pensacola News Journal.*

Dear Mom and Dad,

How's life in P'cola town? I hope things are going well for y'all. Please don't worry too much.

So far, we have not seen too much action except for aircraft and Scud missile alerts. I'm sure we'll begin head-to-head with the Republican Guard in a couple of days. I'm scared to death, but I'm tired of the head games. I'm ready for the challenge.

We have been real busy since the 16th of January. We have been doing a lot of maintenance of equipment and weapons systems, getting them ready to go. We have been moving every day for the past week to keep the Iraqis from finding out where we are. Believe me, we are a lot closer than they want us to be.

How do I feel just days before going into action, you ask?

It feels like game week and we are just getting ready to play Choctawhatchee.

You train hard.

You study your opponent's plays.

You prepare your equipment.

You get the "pep talks."

Friday night you strap on the pads, put on the cleats, and run out in the bright stadium lights.

It feels exactly like that. The nervousness, the nausea, its exactly the same. Except I don't have to worry about Coach Carl Madison. Ha, ha.

I hope this is over soon. I'm so sick of this place.

I will write as much as possible. PRAY.

I love you,

Tim

Tim Thomas was just days away from his division beginning artillery raids when he wrote that letter and would remain in the area until late April of 1991. In the late 1990s, he served as part of a search and recovery team that went to North Korea and recovered the remains of nine U.S. Servicemen lost in the Korean War. In 2003, he returned to the Middle East as part of the invasion of Iraq and the capture of Baghdad.

Tim finally retired from the Army as a Lieutenant Colonel in 2010 after serving for twenty-three years. He started the Junior Reserve Officers' Training Corps (JROTC) program at Viera High School in Melbourne, Florida and now serves on the city council of Melbourne. His biography on the city's website proudly mentions that he played for legendary high school football coach Carl Madison.

Thomas credits Madison with instilling many lessons that helped him achieve success over the years, such as understanding that every day is a competition. And if you didn't produce, you would be replaced. He credits his work ethic and mental toughness to the time spent under the tutelage of Madison.

CHAPTER SIX

TRIUMPHANT RETURN

FOLLOWING HIS DISMISSAL from Tate High School, Madison wanted to continue working in the school system in some capacity so he could keep adding years towards his retirement. He called School Superintendent Charlie Stokes, and Stokes told Madison that he would take care of him.

Madison quickly got a job as a visiting teacher and the offensive coordinator at Pensacola High School under Leo Carvalis. The visiting teacher position only required that he check on kids being out of school and other minimal things.

"Hell, people didn't know where I was half the time. I'd go to New Orleans to the racetrack. But I got my work done," Madison said.

Madison served in the role for two years until he was named head coach at Ernest Ward in Walnut Hill, Florida where he began as a head coach back in 1957. The school also named him its athletic director.

Principal H. Eugene Pettis said he was "pleased to have someone with [Madison's] experience taking charge of the program, and we're looking for positive things to come out of this."

Madison said of the hiring and move to the small school Ernest Ward, "Coaching is coaching. You still put in the same amount of hours, and it's just as important at the small schools as it is at the bigger schools, and I've coached them all."

Coming off a 1–9 record in 1984, the Ernest Ward High School football program had not experienced success to any significant degree in many years. For Madison it provided an opportunity to return to running the show. He believed he still had a lot to offer as a head coach. Plus, he still needed at least four more years in the Florida system to begin collecting retirement.

Ernest Ward opened season by defeating Vernon 37–6, matching the previous season's victory total in their first game. They followed that up by beating Cottondale 68–0 with Madison's Golden Eagles rushing for 401 yards. The offense came back to earth the next week in a 12–0 loss to Flomaton.

A big rivalry contest with Century came next, made even more interesting since it was a battle between Carl Madison and Roy Roberts, who not that long ago faced off against each other as the head coaches of Tate and Pine Forest. The series between Ernest Ward and Century dated back to 1949.

"You've got kin people in Walnut Hill and kin people in Century. They're not far across from here," Madison said. Just over a decade later, the two schools consolidated to become Northview High School.

Madison had confidence in his team. He believed they were a completely different group from the one he inherited. Though he would coach them in practice the way he had coached all of his previous teams, running plays over and over until the players were precise in their execution, there were other areas he focused on with this Ernest Ward group. Things that would benefit them the rest of their lives.

"The big thing is teaching them pride and poise and to keep a cool head at all times. There's great spirit and attitude. The changes are going the right way," he said.

A year previously, a one-loss Century team dominated a one-win Ernest Ward squad. But in 1985, the Eagles stayed with the Blackcats from start to finish before eventually falling 14–10.

The Golden Eagles returned to the win column when they defeated

J.U. Blacksher of Uriah, Alabama—the town of Carl Madison's birth—
by a score of 36–0 to move their record to 3–2. Victories over Castleber-
ry, Alabama Conecuh County, Frisco City, and Freeport came over the
next four weeks. The victory over Freeport raised Ernest Ward's record to
6–2, which exceeded the total number of victories for the school in the
past three years combined.

Next came a matchup with Baker, winners of thirty-two straight and
two-time defending state champions. In recent years, Ernest Ward could
not compete with the Gators, but they battled them on this evening. The
Eagles came within a touchdown in the third quarter before eventually
falling 28–12.

"We didn't play as well as we could have played," Madison said, once
again using *we* to avoid *they* and singling out the players. "But I'm proud
of the boys. And the three losses we have are nothing to be ashamed
about."

The Golden Eagles closed out the season with a dominating 56–0
defeat of Jay to run their record to 7–3, a remarkable turnaround from
the one-win season the year before Madison arrived. He again proved
how exceptional he was as a high school football coach. In a very short
time, he completely changed the attitude of his players. They gained confidence in themselves, believed in what they were doing, and expected
good things to happen. Their final record reflected the dramatic change.

Madison once again demonstrated his ability to completely change
the fortunes of a football program, and it looked as though he could continue his success at Ernest Ward for many years to come. But given that
he had proven he could win on the largest stage in one of the top states
for high school football in the country, it was difficult to imagine he
would pass up an opportunity to return to such a stage. That opportunity
did not take long to appear, and it presented itself in an unexpected way
and through a person one would least suspect. Things were about to get
very interesting again in Pensacola-area high school football.

By the mid-1970s, three Pensacola-area high schools, Tate,
Woodham, and Escambia, had all grown to over three thousand stu-

dents, and the determination was made that another high school was needed to alleviate the overcrowding. The school eventually added was built on Long Leaf Drive and named Pine Forest High School for the area it was located. It opened its doors in the fall of 1975.

It wasn't long before the Pine Forest Eagles football team began experiencing success. After a couple of state runner-up finishes in 1978 and 1979 the Eagles faltered and saw their district rivals, Tate and Woodham win three state championships between them from 1980 to 1985.

Ralph Godwin, the principal at Tate who forced Madison's resignation in 1983, was named principal of Pine Forest High School in 1986. Godwin wanted a coach who could return the Eagles to their prior glory and get them to the pinnacle of Florida high school football. So, he placed a call to Carl Madison asking him to come to his office for a visit.

They did not have a long conversation. According to Madison, it began with an invitation.

"Carl, how do you feel about working for me again?" Godwin asked.

"I told you that you made a mistake when you fired me," Madison responded.

Godwin said, "Well I want you to work for me."

Grace Madison questioned whether it was a good idea to work for Godwin again considering how things ended at Tate.

"Ralph realized he made a mistake," Madison said.

Although he was proud, he could be forgiving. And he wasn't about to let anything prevent him from going somewhere he felt he could win big. He accepted the offer and returned to the big time in Florida high school football.

On leaving Ernest Ward after just one season there, Madison said, "It's a great school. They're great people to work with. The only reason I'm leaving is to get back down in the center circle."

Madison departed amicably. Though his returning players were certainly disappointed, if they were honest with themselves, like everyone else in the area, they had to understand the move.

Madison chose not to insert himself in the search for his replacement. His focus was now completely on Pine Forest. After approximately ten applicants for the coaching role at Ernest Ward were considered, the offer was made to Blair Armstrong, the head coach of Washington High School. Armstrong did the exact opposite of Madison, leaving a much larger school for a smaller one. He had won a state championship at Monticello Jefferson County, an AA school, in 1982 and just preferred that type of atmosphere and lifestyle for his family.

Regarding the move to Pine Forest, Madison told the *Pensacola News Journal*, "I think they have a good school there. When I was at Tate, we got our better athletes from the Pine Forest area before they split off." And with a portent of things to come he went on to say, "Any of the players that want to move over into our district are welcome. We'll be glad to have them. We need a lot of help."

Madison inherited a young football team at Pine Forest. Although the Eagles' record in 1985 was a respectable 7–3, they returned only four starters from that team. He attempted to temper expectations heading into the 1986 season.

"We're not big at all. But size is not everything. You can't waste time wishing for what you don't have. You have to do what you can with what you've got," Madison stated.

Rodney Blunt was a sophomore on the 1986 team. He attended Pensacola High School his freshman year, but his family later moved into the Pine Forest district. Over the summer, Madison showed up at the Blunt house to introduce himself as the new head coach of the Eagles. Blunt had no interest in leaving PHS or playing for Madison, and the coach's visit did not change that.

When Madison left, Blunt made his way as quickly as possible to Pensacola High to visit their head football coach Leo Carvalis to see if he could figure out a way to stay and play for him. When he got to Carvalis' office, he saw Madison sitting there.

"I couldn't get away from him," Blunt said later. The family ultimately decided Blunt would play at Pine Forest due to the location of their new residence, and Rodney ended up being extremely happy things worked out the way they did.

Madison's first game as the head coach of Pine Forest found him facing Tate, the school that brought him his greatest glory as a coach, and the one he believed had wrongly let him go. There was no question he badly wanted to win this one.

Things looked bleak for the Eagles when they trailed 26–14 in the third quarter. But when Marquette Oliver returned a punt eighty yards for a touchdown, it became a ballgame. Pine Forest got the ball with less than two minutes to play, and quarterback John Brown drove them to the Tate forty-yard line. From there he threw two long passes that were knocked down in the end zone, and Tate prevailed 26–21.

Losses to Fort Walton Beach, Panama City Rutherford, and Panama City Mosley followed. For the first time in his coaching career, a Madison team began the season 0–4. At that point, everyone associated with the program needed a win.

Next on the schedule came Washington, a school that had never defeated Pine Forest. The Eagles fell behind 7–0 early, but a John Brown touchdown evened the score. After second and third quarter field goals gave the Wildcats a 13–7 lead, touchdowns in the third and fourth quarter by running back Mondo Miller provided Pine Forest with all the scoring they needed in a 21–13 victory.

Against Milton, the Eagles were one play away from stretching their winning streak to two, but Panther kicker Chris Herring kicked a forty-one-yard field goal with two seconds left to lift his team to a 9–7 win.

Then came a matchup with Woodham. The Titans were shockingly winless on the season just a year removed from losing in the 5-A state championship game and after winning two state titles in the prior three years. Pine Forest kept them winless by handling the Titans easily, 46–16.

After being completely overmatched and losing to Pensacola High, the Eagles travelled to Niceville for a contest most expected them to lose. They trailed 10–3 into the fourth quarter but rallied on scores from Mondo Miller and Rodney Blunt to win 17–10.

Madison's squad had the not so good fortune of playing Escambia in their season finale. It was also Emmitt Smith's final regular season contest as a high school football player. The Gators were two-time defending state champions and were ranked the number one team in the country just a week earlier before being upset by PHS, meaning there would be no playoffs for them this year, though they would play in a bowl at the season's conclusion. Smith came in as the second leading rusher in the history of high school football.[8]

Escambia dominated the Eagles 48–7, dropping Pine Forest's final record to 3–7. Smith did not carry the ball much but still managed to gain over one hundred yards rushing. It would not have been particularly memorable were it not for how things ended. With his team leading 45–7, Escambia coach Dwight Thomas called timeout with seconds remaining and kicked a forty-yard field goal to add to the final score, supposedly just to give his kicker some practice.

Madison wasn't convinced nor happy. He gathered his coaches afterwards and told them, "By God I hope every one of you is back next year."

There would be payback eventually.

Before the 1987 season, Madison's team suffered a number of setbacks. A few of the projected starters decided they no longer wanted to play football. A starting defender moved out of state. It was also discovered that a key running back repeated the tenth grade and no longer had any eligibility left. Another running back suffered a knee injury.

Despite the setbacks, Madison still felt he had a good football team. But the district was extremely tough. Entering the season, Washington was the number one 5A team in Florida and ranked number three nationally, while Panama City Mosley was the second-ranked team in the state. Beating either one of them would be a fantastic accomplishment, but the Eagles had other games to worry about before facing those two.

Jerry Pollard served as the defensive coordinator during Madison's years at Pine Forest. He became the Eagles' head coach when Madison departed and led the team to a state championship in 2000. Despite the

---

8   Smith ended his football playing days as the all-time leading rusher in the NFL and
     a three-time Super Bowl champion.

poor record of the previous season, he wasn't concerned and did not see any concern in Madison either.

"There was not a lot of difference [in Madison's attitude] in 3–7 and 9–1. We worked hard," Pollard said.

Though the losing seasons were few during Madison's coaching career, when a new season began it made no difference to him. Nor did coming off a winning one. He focused on the present and his current team. In fact, that focus typically began days—if not immediately—after a season ended.

Another assistant coach on the 1987 Pine Forest squad was Madison's quarterback from his 1980 Tate state championship team, Keith Leonard. Leonard now served on the Pine Forest varsity staff after having led the freshman team to a 7–0 record in 1986. He was responsible for the quarterbacks and running backs.

Leonard always sat behind Madison on the team bus as a player, and he continued that practice as a coach. He still recalls a time on the bus following a big win at Pine Forest. While most celebrated, he sat quietly in his usual seat on the second row behind Madison, thinking about what he needed to do in preparation for the next game.

Madison recognized what he was doing and told him, "Today, you've become a football coach."

Leonard applied a great deal of what he learned from Madison when he later served as head coach at Tate. He emulated Madison's practice schedules and how he prepared his team. He made sure he stayed flexible enough to work with the talent he had and would not impose one particular system if it didn't match the skill sets of his players, not because he preferred one offense or defense over another.

But in 1987, that remained a few years away.

Madison's Pine Forest Eagles opened the 1987 season against the Tate Aggies. It was his first appearance as an opposing coach at Tate's Pete Gindl Stadium since being let go there almost five years ago.

"It will be nice to see old friends, but I still want to win. Winning is what it's all about," Madison stated.

Madison began by ordering an onside kick. Though unsuccessful, Tate fumbled two plays later, the Eagles recovered, and they drove into field goal range where Rodney Allen made the kick to give them a 3–0 lead. Madison then ordered another onside kick which Pine Forest did recover. John Brown led the team on a six-play drive, finishing it off with a one-yard run to give the Eagles a 9–0 lead on their way to a 16–0 victory. Then came a fairly routine 28–14 win over Fort Walton Beach. Sophomore running back, Anthony Toler, who transferred from Tate after his freshman season, led the Eagles with 196 yards rushing against the Vikings.

Next came Pensacola High. The Tigers beat Pine Forest 45–10 the year before and were ranked number one in the Florida 4A poll.

Pensacola High School coach Leo Carvalis did not expect another mismatch. "They are a good-looking team. They're 2–0 and have done a lot of things right. But we're not going to change anything for them. We're going to relax and go out and play our game," he said.

Madison, ever the strategist, surprised PHS by coming out in a full-house backfield. The Eagles jumped out to a 14–0 first quarter lead but couldn't hang on, eventually falling 21–14.

"We may have underestimated them," Carvalis said.

Though the loss was deflating, it prefaced the beginning of something very special. Something that Pine Forest fans still talk about.

The schedule did not get any easier for Pine Forest when they traveled to face district foe Panama City Mosley, the second-rated team in Florida Class 5A and eleventh-rated team in the country according to *USA Today*. Of the eight staff members from the *Pensacola News Journal* picking the games, only one of them, Mark Bullock, predicted the Eagles to prevail.

It was an exciting contest. The Dolphins took a 3–0 lead in the first quarter on a thirty-seven-yard field goal. Pine Forest responded with a touchdown pass from John Brown to Jason Davis to go up 7–3. Mosley scored before the half though and took a 10–7 lead into the locker room. John Brown threw another scoring strike in the third quarter, this time to tight end David Chisenhall, and the Eagles led 14–10. Mosley responded with a punt return in the fourth quarter for a 16–14 lead.

It remained that way until late in the game. Three plays after the Dolphins fumbled on their own seven-yard line, Ronnie Sonnier plunged in for the final touchdown, and Madison's Pine Forest Eagles had a stunning 21–16 victory.

Madison offered a low-key explanation for his team's amazing performance. "We have a pretty good football team. I think we're kind of getting it together."

The win vaulted Pine Forest into the state 5A top ten at number four. But it was not the time to celebrate given that an even bigger matchup came next.

It is difficult to imagine a team in the history of high school football facing a tougher regular season stretch than the three-game gauntlet Pine Forest saw early in the 1987 season. It began with the loss to the Florida number one ranked 4A team, Pensacola High School. Next came a defeat of the Florida 5A number two ranked and eleventh ranked nationally Panama City Mosley Dolphins. It finished with the biggest of all, the Florida 5A number one ranked and number two nationally ranked Washington Wildcats. This time, two of the eight staff members of the *Pensacola News Journal* predicted a Pine Forest victory; Mark Bullock went with the Eagles again and John Donovan joined him.

Washington's head coach Jimmy Nichols, who coached with Madison at Tate, stated what many coaches most likely felt over the years when facing a Carl Madison squad, "I'd feel good if it was just a matchup of personnel. But Carl has so many tricks up his sleeve and uses so many formations . . . he's impossible to prepare for."

Nichols just echoed what so many opposing coaches felt over the years having to coach against Madison. The word "genius" can certainly be overused, but there was no question that some felt that he was an offensive coaching genius. Given limited practice time it was extremely difficult to prepare just for what you expected Madison might throw at you, not to mention he could very possibly have his team do something you've never seen one of his teams do before.

Madison responded to Nichols' comment, "I work hard and believe I'm able to coach from the field. But I don't do anything special."

Washington's Wildcats possessed plenty of incentive coming in. It was crucial to their hopes of a district title, and they had never defeated Pine Forest.

The previous year's loss still stung Washington coach Nichols. "Last year we flat underestimated them. We scored on the second play of the game, and the kids started counting the money. This year, I guarantee you we'll be ready. We'll have a few surprises for them."

According to Jerry Pollard, when Washington got off the bus, Coach Nichols saw one of the Pine Forest ball boys whose father was one of the coaches. "Tell your dad we're going to whip his ass," Nichols said.

The contest took place in front of a raucous crowd at Pine Forest's Lon Wise Stadium. The Eagles struck first with Rodney Blunt bowling into the end zone from the one-yard line. With just over seven minutes left in the first quarter, Pine Forest led 7–0. The Wildcats scored in the second quarter, but a botched extra-point attempt left the score 7–6 in favor of the Eagles at the half. It looked like Washington was taking over when backup tailback Tyrone Bryant scored from three yards out to give the Wildcats a 12–7 lead on the first play of the fourth quarter. With less than seven minutes remaining, the Eagles found themselves trailing and eighty yards from the end zone.

"Get up because we've got to do it now," Rodney Blunt said to his offensive teammates.

The Eagles began to move the ball, but it looked like the drive might stall before a big pass interference call on Washington set Pine Forest up on the Wildcats' thirty-seven. Madison then called a reverse which Robert Grimsley ran to the Washington seven. With 1:41 left on the clock, Blunt drove into the end zone to give the Eagles a 13–12 lead. Washington got one final chance to score but could get no further than their own thirty-nine-yard line.

The Eagles had done it again, and in the process, gave Madison his two-hundredth victory.

"The whole key is believing in yourself, and we did that tonight. We beat an awful good football team. But we're a pretty good team, too," Madison said.

When the next 5A Florida Sports Writers Association high school football poll was released, Pine Forest was number one.

Mike Bennett, Madison's former Tate running back, served as assistant coach on the Washington squad at the time and would later achieve much success as a head coach in the area. He guided Pensacola High to a state championship in 2009 and took Escambia to the finals in 2019. After the devastating loss for the Wildcats, he drove one of the team busses back to Washington, but before they could get off the Pine Forest property, it broke down. He had to walk into the Pine Forest locker room during a tremendous celebration by the team to request assistance from Madison. It was not a pleasant experience for him, he later recalled.

Victories over Milton and Panama City Rutherford followed before a 34–14 win over Choctawhatchee clinched the district title. Pine Forest went to the playoffs for the first time since 1979.

A happy Carl Madison said, "This really feels great. It's great for the boys and for the coaches who've worked so hard this year."

After defeating a winless Woodham squad, the final contest of the regular season featured a matchup with Escambia and head coach Dwight Thomas who called a timeout the year before with a 45–7 lead so he could kick a field goal against Madison's Eagles. The Gators took their opening possession and drove into field goal range, but Marquette Oliver blocked their attempt. Pine Forest then came out with a five receiver, no running back offense, drove down the field and scored, never looking back in a 27–0 revenge-fueled defeat of the Gators. Anthony Toler rushed for 146 yards and three touchdowns. With last year's memory in mind, Madison called timeout at the end of the game to attempt a seventy-plus-yard field goal with obviously no chance of success. Thomas definitely received the message.

During the week Pine Forest prepared for their first playoff matchup, the exciting news came that the Eagles cracked the *USA Today* top twenty-five national rankings at number twenty-five. Gainesville Buchholz came in with only a 6–4 record but winners of six of their last seven following a 0–3 start. They were led by one of the state's top coaches, Al Werneke, who had a 209-66-4 record.

On paper, it looked like the Eagles should cruise, but Madison was having none of that. "You don't assume anything this time of year. This is a new season, a one-game season. Both teams know they have to win to keep playing," he said.

Great coaches don't rely on what has occurred previously and are able to focus on one game at a time.

It appeared to be over early when Pine Forest scored on four of its first five possessions and led 29–0 at the half. But in the second half the Eagles lost three fumbles, and when Buchholz scored with 3:02 left, what was once a 35–0 lead now stood at 35–27. Buchholz got the ball one final time with an opportunity to tie with a touchdown and two-point conversion, but an interception by Al Jackson with 1:33 left put an end to the rally.

The section championship pitted Pine Forest against a 10–1 Jacksonville Sandalwood team. The Saints had only allowed two touchdowns the entire season and shutout six of their opponents.

"That's a heck of a defense. When you only allow two touchdowns all year—that's something," Madison commented.

Things didn't look promising early on as Sandalwood jumped out to a 14–0 lead early in the second quarter. The Eagles responded by scoring on their next four possessions over the second and third quarters. Rodney Blunt pounded the vaunted Saint defense for 243 yards on only eighteen carries. Possibly the biggest play of the year occurred with only thirty seconds left in the half when Blunt ran seventy-one yards for a touchdown to tie the score at 14–14, a backbreaking play that completely changed the momentum going into halftime. Early in the third quarter, Blunt added another touchdown on a forty-seven-yard run down the left sideline, giving the Eagles their first lead at 20–14, and Pine Forest scored again in the third quarter. Sandalwood answered late to cut the margin to 27–21, but when Spook Morrow recovered the Saints onside kick, the Eagles only needed to run out the clock. They did—and advanced to the semifinals.

Spook Morrow, the only senior starting offensive lineman on the Eagle squad, stood five foot eight and weighed 205 pounds. Against Sandalwood, he faced off with a six foot seven, 215-pound defensive lineman.

"He was laughing at me in the beginning," Morrow commented. "But he wasn't laughing at the end. He was upset. Their whole team was."

The now fifteenth nationally ranked Eagles saw a semifinal that brought the Bradenton Manatee Hurricanes to Lon Wise Stadium. The Hurricanes had won two of the last four Florida largest school classification state championships, including the 1985 one over Woodham. But they were no match for Pine Forest who came away with a 22–0 victory, sending the Eagles to their first state championship game since 1979.

Defensive coordinator Jerry Pollard later said about Manatee, "They had a big mouth coach. He ran his mouth, and he had no chance after that."

The state championship found the Eagles facing the 12–1 Dunedin Falcons.

John Brown spoke of his desire to be a champion. "I've always wanted to have one of those rings on my finger. I can remember when Escambia won those state titles, and all of their players had those state championship rings to show off. That's the first thing I would notice when I was around them. Now we've got the chance to get our own. And ours would be newer."

Pine Forest held the number one ranking while Dunedin was fifth. The Falcons had the advantage of playing in front of their home crowd. In addition, they returned almost every starter from a team that lost in the state finals to Lakeland the previous year. In contrast to the multiple-set, offensive attack employed by Pine Forest, the Falcons ran a no option, wishbone attack. In their prior two playoff contests, Dunedin only attempted one pass in each.

Dunedin's coach Ken Weir offered high praise for Madison and the Eagles. "Controlling the ball will be a big factor to defend against all their craziness. They line up in some stuff I couldn't call if I wanted to— our kids wouldn't understand. It's the best coached team I've ever seen."

Madison showed some concern during the week. "I'm afraid our youth might tell. It's a big game and a long trip [five hundred miles], and for a lot of our kids, this is their first time away from home."

Although significant for the players and coaches, it was also significant for the community. It had been almost a decade since Pine Forest lost consecutive state championship games to Merritt Island, and in the meantime, fans of the Eagles witnessed local teams—Tate, Woodham, and Escambia—all win state championships. They hoped it was their turn.

Madison reflected on his previous state championship with Tate in 1980 and wanted the same for his current group. "This isn't for me. I've been there. I hope we can win this one for the boys and other coaches so they can share the feeling."

His comments shed light on his perspective as a coach: he certainly loved to win, but he also loved seeing those who had put in an incredible amount of work and effort get to experience the highest levels of success and all that came with it.

The Eagles weren't going to play conservatively and proved that early on when tight end Jason Davis threw a thirty-five-yard pass to David Chisenhall to get them to the Falcons one-yard line. The Falcon defense held, but kicker Michael Crites kicked a twenty-one-yard field goal to give Pine Forest a 3–0 first quarter lead. In the second quarter, John Brown delivered a screen pass to Anthony Toler who went nineteen yards for a score. Crites added the extra point to make it 10–0 Eagles.

"I felt like I had to make a big play. I saw a little peep, and all I was thinking was endzone," Toler said afterwards.

It remained 10–0 Pine Forest until the fourth quarter. With 6:10 left, Toler added his second touchdown, and the lead increased to 17–0.

Rodney Blunt added a final score, and when the whistle blew, Pine Forest had won its first state championship 24–0.

"Our passing game clicked extremely well," said Madison. "We could do more things on offense than they could do. That was the difference." When asked to compare his current squad to the 1980 state championship team he coached at Tate High School, Madison said, "They were both pretty good."

Defensive coordinator Jerry Pollard had plenty of reason to be proud of his players. "We really play together more as a team than we do with ability. I don't think anyone had more togetherness than we [did]," he commented. "I think we showed that tonight. We played together as one." The Dunedin offense gained just eighty-six yards, with most of that coming in the final two minutes.

Pollard singled out two of his defensive players who played hurt, Steve Kaderly and Wade Chavers. "Kaderly has a torn discus in his knee and hasn't practiced in three weeks. He only plays on Friday nights and shows amazing courage. Wade sprained his ankle this week and couldn't walk. It shows you how hard our guys wanted to win."

Kaderly registered an amazing twenty-three tackles.

At 1:00 in the morning, a few hours after leading his team to the state title, all John Brown could think about was going home. "I'll feel better when I can get home and brag about this," he said. "Not too many people around here know us. I'll feel even better when I get back to town and order those [championship] rings."

John Hammack, a defensive lineman on the team who went on to become a medical doctor, later said that being on that team and what they accomplished was still a big deal to him. "In my travels, I've never met anyone else who was on a state championship team," he said.

In the final *USA Today* national high school rankings, Pine Forest finished at number twelve. John Brown received first-team quarterback honors on the Florida 5-A squad and was named the Northwest Florida Offensive Player of the Year. David Chisenhall, Marquette Oliver, and Steve Kaderly were named to the Northwest Florida 1st team. Carl

Madison added another Northwest Florida Coach of the Year award to his collection.

His legend continued to grow.

While coaching at Pine Forest with Madison, Keith Leonard got to see another side of the man. Madison liked to laugh. He wanted his coaching staff to have fun and not talk football 24/7. He built comradery among them. He also talked to the coaches about the expectations he had for them just as he did with players. He expected fellowship, brotherhood, loyalty, and that they would outwork their opposing coaching staffs. He also emphasized the community's expectations for the program and how important it was that they lived up to them.

Occasionally, Madison told the coaches that the Quarterback Club provided additional funds, and he'd give them one hundred dollars to take out their wives or girlfriends or do something for their kids. Leonard never knew if the money really came from the Quarterback Club or from Madison's pocket. Either way, there was little doubt Madison had something to do with it.

Madison possessed an uncanny ability to see coaching talent that others might not recognize. He always kept someone on staff who handled paperwork well since it wasn't something he wanted to spend a lot of time on. He knew that person played a vital role in the success of the team. He made other coaches on his staff successful. It was alright if you didn't know certain things. He would teach you what you needed to know.

He also gave his coaches confidence because he possessed such a great football mind. He could dissect a defense. He looked for "the bubble" or "triangle" where there might be a weakness, and he game planned to attack that. He could anticipate what adjustments an opposing defense might make. Though he ran a minimal number of plays, he would figure out how to outnumber the defense, out position them through formations to get the other team to line up where he wanted them to line up. Occasionally, he lined his offense in some type of wild formation early, just to see how the opposing team would respond.

As a player, Leonard knew that Madison sometimes did things to help young men in need, but he didn't realize the extent of what he did until he coached with him. Sometimes Madison would give players a ride home. He would spend time with the parents talking about their sons. While at Pine Forest, a player's house burned down, and Madison quickly organized some relief. He took up a collection of money, clothing, and other items to give to the family. He helped other families in need also. Due to that and many other instances, the parents trusted him. It wasn't that Madison treated all their boys equally. He never claimed to do so, though he did treat them all fairly.

There are few better ways to pay tribute to someone than to name a child after that person. That is what Keith Leonard and his wife Melinda did when they named their second daughter Madison before the name reached its current level of popularity. When they found out they were having a girl, Melinda suggested the name because of the impact Carl Madison had made on their family. Beyond coaching Keith and later hiring him as a coach, Carl and his wife Grace gave the young couple a week in their timeshare in south Florida and were generous to them in numerous ways. When they called him to tell him they were naming their girl after him, he was extremely touched.

In the years that followed, he always asked Keith about his family members and finished up with "How is 'my' Madison?"

As the Eagles prepared for the 1988 season, everything should have been perfect. They were coming off a state championship the prior year and many key players returned. But a cloud hung over the team. The school was fined five hundred dollars, and Madison was suspended for five days by the Florida High School Activities Association for violating bylaw 12-7-2 Note 1, which prohibits recruiting.

The incident in question involved a visit Madison made to Pensacola High School quarterback Tyrone Roberts in August, prior to the season. Madison maintained that his visit was to clear up residency requirements with the parents. According to Keith Leonard, Roberts lived in the Pine Forest district, and he and Madison visited with his family to determine why he attended PHS. Madison appealed the suspension, and the hearing was scheduled for October 18. The season started with the hearing looming in the background, but Madison did not allow it to distract him. In fact, Madison and Pine Forest prepared a loophole if the suspension stood. He would serve the five days during one of the team's two open weeks and therefore not miss a game or any game week practices.

That proved unnecessary when on October 18 the Escambia County School Board voted unanimously to overturn the suspension.

Madison commented, "They didn't have a case against me. I think they [the school board] had all the facts and went by the facts."

Pine Forest entered the 1988 season ranked first in Florida and number six nationally by *USA Today*—no surprise given that the Eagles returned fourteen starters from their 1987 championship team. At the same time, Madison understood the difficulty of repeating as champions. After his 1980 championship season at Tate, the Aggies failed to make the playoffs in 1981.

"There's a tendency to feel you don't have to work as hard the following year because of the hard work put in the year before. The kids have to understand the other team is working twice as hard to knock you off," Madison commented.

Rodney Blunt was a senior now and being recruited by a number of big-time college football programs. The young man who did not want to play for Carl Madison two years earlier now recognized that Madison had made him a better running back. Blunt later explained that at one point Madison told him he should go into a dark, four-cornered room and sit in the middle while going over the playbook in his head. Blunt did that while visualizing the plays and his own performance. He would get plenty of opportunities to play all of that out on the field in 1988.

The first team that the Eagles faced in what proved a historic 1988 season was Madison's former team, the Tate Aggies. Anthony Toler and Rodney Blunt both rushed for over one hundred yards in a 16–6 Pine Forest win. The Eagles had an easier time the next week, defeating Fort Walton Beach 35–3.

Game three found Pine Forest taking on Pensacola High School, the lone team to defeat them the previous season. It was a huge matchup in the area, featuring two number one teams, since the Tigers were top rated in 4A.

"We don't want to play ourselves out against Pensacola High then have nothing left for Mosley and Washington. We can't get too keyed up for this game," Madison said.

The Eagles made it clear they were now the dominant team in the city, exploding for twenty-one points in a sixty-two-second span of the first quarter to effectively end things. They cruised the rest of the way to a 40–0 victory.

A 39–0 defeat of Panama City Mosley led into a matchup with a revenge-seeking Washington. Were it not for a 13–12 loss to Pine Forest the prior year, the Wildcats might be the ones defending a state title. That was not forgotten by Washington players or its head coach.

"All our kids have been concerned with is last year when they beat us and kept us from making the playoffs. Now our kids want to keep them from going," said Washington coach Jimmy Nichols.

The Wildcats were far from the team of 1987. Their top two running backs sat out with injuries, and they sported only a 2–2 record.

Madison thought that worked in the Wildcats' favor. "Washington will come with everything trying to whip us. If we're not ready, they can do it."

Al Jackson scored an early touchdown that ended up the only one of the contest as Pine Forest escaped 12–3. The Eagles achieved their twelfth straight victory in the series.

Dejected Washington coach Jimmy Nichols commented, "We beat them everywhere but on the scoreboard. It's the same ol' story when Washington plays Pine Forest."

In fact, the Eagles certainly didn't play their best, turning the ball over five times, but they outgained the Wildcats 184–127.

Pine Forest defensive coordinator Jerry Pollard said of the strong defensive performance, "We were tough tonight. It's absolutely the best effort I've ever seen. Our intensity was something else."

Years later when it was pointed out to Pollard that Nichols made the comment about beating them everywhere but on the scoreboard, he said, "They couldn't have scored if we were still playing."

A dominating 50–7 defeat of Milton gave Pine Forest a 6–0 record and increased their overall win streak to seventeen, the longest active streak in the state of Florida. With it, the Eagles moved to number four in the *USA Today* national rankings.

Pine Forest had an opportunity to wrap up the district championship against Choctawhatchee the next week, and it was a severe test. Early on, everything appeared to be going as planned for the Eagles when they opened up a 22–0 lead, but Choctaw blocked an Eagle punt and scored just before halftime to cut the deficit to 22–7. In the third quarter, the Indians scored twice to tie the score at 22–22. Then as time expired in the third quarter, Indian kicker Eric McBryde kicked a fifty-eight-yard field goal to put Choctaw in front 25–22.

When they entered the fourth quarter, Pine Forest trailed for the first time all season. Not only was their national ranking in jeopardy, but a loss would severely damage their chances of even going to the state playoffs. On the fifth play of the ensuing drive, Anthony Toler ran thirty-three yards for a score, and when Toler also converted the two-point conversion, the Eagles were up 30–25. After stopping Choctaw, the Eagles drove for another score on their next series and prevailed 37–25. It clinched the district title and another berth in the state playoffs.

Madison said, "We won, and that's all I care about. I'm not satisfied with the way we played, but a win is a win. We showed a little character after falling behind. I was really proud that we did it [scored] twice in a row."

Indians coach Lionel Fayard summed up his thoughts. "We had them on the ropes, but they responded. I guess that's what great teams do. They make the big plays."

No drama occurred in the Eagles 60–0 defeat of Woodham. They remained ranked number one in Florida Class 5A and number four in the national rankings from *USA Today*. While hopes of a possible national championship remained, the odds were slim that the three teams above them would all lose with so few games remaining in the season.

The ninth contest of the season found Pine Forest facing the Escambia Gators. Escambia won two state championships in the decade of the 1980s. But those were the Gators of Emmitt Smith, and this team was not near as talented.

If 60–0 over Woodham seemed like a blowout, it had nothing on what occurred against Escambia. The final score was 93–14 in the Eagles' favor. Remarkably, it could have been worse, but Madison played his reserves almost the entire second half after the first team ran up fifty-one points in the opening half. It was one of the four greatest routs in Escambia County history and the biggest since 1928 when Pensacola High School defeated Robertsdale, Alabama 110–0. Anthony Toler and Rodney Blunt each gained over one hundred yards rushing in the first half to lead the Eagles.

Madison praised his team but wanted to make it clear the Eagles did not try to run up the score. "We looked good. We scored that many points because we had help from the other team. They threw some incomplete passes; we had a punt return for a touchdown and a blocked punt. They had as much to do with it, they gave us a lot of opportunities."

There is a tendency for coaches to focus on their top players to the detriment of the rest of the squad, but that was not how Madison operated. He recognized the importance of rewarding everyone who made the sacrifices on a daily basis that were necessary to have a successful program.

Regarding Madison's general thoughts on running up the score, he believed you should try to score whenever you could, no matter the score or time remaining. But you did so with your second and third-team players if the game was out of hand. They worked hard and deserved the opportunity to try to score when they played. It meant something to them and to their parents. It was nice for the parents to see their son score. Madison only considered it unsportsmanlike if you left your starters in late during a blowout and continued to try to put up points. Because he held to that philosophy in the Pine Forest game, he did not consider it unsportsmanlike.

Dwight Thomas, coach of the Gators since the glory days of Emmitt Smith, demonstrated class when he said, "They've got a great team, and they did a great job tonight. But I'm proud to be a Gator," he said. "I hope Pine Forest wins the state championship. I'm pulling for them all the way."

Later when asked specifically if Pine Forest ran up the score, Thomas responded, "I would never say that. You can never tell your team to stop or slow down. They were just a very good football team that was hitting on all cylinders."

Years later when asked about Thomas saying he hoped Pine Forest would go on to be state champions, Madison replied, "He was lying." Madison also said that he didn't really get into coaching rivalries and that he just wanted to win. He did acknowledge however, that the game against Escambia and Dwight Thomas might have been different. He also admitted, "If I had known what the record was, we would have gone ahead and broken it."

The state playoffs began the next week, and the Eagles faced a 5–5 Jacksonville Forrest team that won a three-way tiebreaker just to get to the playoffs. Madison was not concerned with the pressure of the state playoffs.

"I don't feel it [pressure], and I don't think the kids do either," he said. "We're in the playoffs now, and this is just another game along the way."

Madison decided to open up the passing game against Forrest. Ronnie Sonnier threw for 169 yards and two touchdowns as Pine Forest won handily 50–7. "We always could throw it. We just didn't want to. But we wanted to let other people know we could throw the football," he said.

The second round of the playoffs brought an intriguing matchup with Lake City Columbia. The coach of Columbia was Joe Montgomery, who served as the Pine Forest coach from 1982–1985, the years before

Madison took over. Montgomery compiled a very respectable 26–14 record there but never won a district championship. He decided to leave when Pine Forest hired a new principal, Ralph Godwin, understanding that principals liked to hire their own coaches and knowing that Godwin was the principal at Tate when Madison won the state championship there.

Montgomery was thrilled to coach at Lake City. "There's nothing that can compare to this. As far as I'm concerned, this is one of the best 5A jobs in the state," he commented. On the upcoming matchup, he said, "I always want to look good for my friends. It's kind of like when Carl plays Tate."

The Eagles carried a twenty-one-game win streak into the matchup and easily stretched it to twenty-two. On the second play, Ronnie Sonnier ran forty-eight yards for a score, and they cruised to a 47–6 victory. A dejected Montgomery commented, "They were just a much better football team. Their defense was so outstanding."

More great news arrived the next day when reports came in that incredibly, the top three teams in the *USA Today* high school football poll—Los Angeles Loyola, Sugarland (Texas) Willowridge, and Valdosta Georgia all lost their playoff games. Carl Madison's Pine Forest Eagles were now not only the number one team in Florida, but also the number one team in the country.

Principal Ralph Godwin made the announcement to the school at 1:40 p.m. the next Monday as students, teachers, and administrators all cheered loudly. "Right now, my head is swimming. It's really a great feeling to accomplish this," Godwin said.

Pine Forest senior John Kindergan added, "How many seniors can say they graduated with the top football team in the nation?"

Senior cornerback Al Jackson added some perspective, though when he said, "I'm excited, but I'll be happier if we win state. Polls don't get you [championship] rings."

The Eagles were just two years removed from a 3–7 season. Godwin credited Madison for the turnaround. "He gets more out of his players than any man I know. I don't think there is any doubt that Carl Madison is the best high school football coach in the country."

As he prepared his team to face 11–1 Stuart Martin County in the semifinals, Madison spoke of the opportunity for his team. "We've told them they have a chance to do what no other team in the state has ever done [finish at number one in the *USA Today* poll]. We can look back on that forever. But the kids know this chance might never come along again."

In Stuart Martin County, the Eagles faced an explosive offense that operated from the wing-T. The offense was similar to the wishbone in that it used three running backs and a quarterback, just more compact. Fortunately for Pine Forest, they faced the same kind of offense earlier in the season against Choctawhatchee.

When the Pine Forest players showed up in the locker room on Friday, they found a message inscribed on the wall. "Two games left for an undefeated season and a state championship. Can we do it?" it read. The Eagles set out early to prove that they could. After fumbling on their opening possession, Pine Forest scored touchdowns on the ensuing three. Stuart Martin County scored late, but by then things were completely out of reach and it ended 41–6.

Well-coached players understand how important it was for everyone to play their roles properly if success is going to be achieved. Running back Rodney Blunt demonstrated this in his postgame comments when he said, "Last week the offensive line told me I wasn't going to be touched. I reminded them of that before the game, and they all got fired up. Those guys are great."

The week heading into the state championship matchup with Sarasota Riverview was as intense as any Madison or his players ever experienced. "I get up for every ball game, but this one is really big," said Madison. "There's so much on the line for these kids Friday night. This year is entirely different than last year. We've already won the state championship, and now we're trying to hold onto it and do something even bigger."

For the first time in the playoffs, Pine Forest faced a team of similar size and strength in Sarasota Riverview. They had enjoyed a considerable size advantage against their three previous opponents. One advantage for the Eagles was that the contest was at their own Lon Wise Stadium. On a cool evening, the teams hit the field in front of over ten thousand fans and a live television audience.

Things did not start out well for Pine Forest when they fumbled the ball on their opening possession. Riverview recovered the ball on the Eagle twenty-six-yard line. After gaining nine yards on three plays, they decided to go for it on fourth down but were stopped cold by the Pine Forest defense. The Eagle offense then settled down, marching eighty-four yards in six plays, capped by a touchdown pass from Ronnie Sonnier to Jason Davis. Two plays later, the Eagles recovered a fumble on the Riverview sixteen-yard line. Sonnier rushed into the end zone a couple of plays later to make the score 14–0 Eagles with 2:24 left in the first quarter. The second quarter went just as well when Madison's troops added another pair of scores and headed into the locker room with a 30–0 halftime lead against a team that had only given up thirty-two points all year.

The Eagles played a somewhat sloppy second half, but they did not need to be perfect. Riverview scored three times in the fourth quarter, but 43–27 was as close as they would get. Late in the contest, Pine Forest found themselves deep in Ram territory again. Madison called a timeout and walked into the Eagle huddle. He told running backs Rodney Blunt and Anthony Toler to each pick a number, the one closest to the one he was thinking of would get to carry the ball with an opportunity to score the final touchdown.

Blunt, who already had over one hundred yards rushing and a fifty-seven-yard score, picked closest. But on the play, Toler got the ball and scored for the third time.

Blunt, being a senior, wanted Toler to have the opportunity to score. "I had so much. I knew it would mean more to Toler," Blunt would later say.

With the extra point added, the final margin was 50–27. The Eagles were state champions again—and this time, national champions as well.

Speaking of Blunt's selflessness ten years later Madison said, "It just brings you chills to know you had that type of people at that age. I probably would have scored if I were Rodney. That moment will always be a touching thing to me."

Madison was ecstatic immediately after the victory. "We had to be great tonight and we were. We've been battling adversity all year—that recruiting crap. And we were a target every time we stepped out on the field," he said.

Quarterback Ronnie Sonnier felt particularly vindicated. Earlier in the week, Riverview coach John Sprague commented on a local radio program that he "couldn't believe they [Pine Forest] had come this far with a quarterback that bad."

"I felt I had to prove something," Sonnier said. "My dad heard the comments on the radio and told me a couple of days ago."

Madison said, "I think Ronnie showed why he's the most underrated player in the state of Florida."

The final statistics of the Eagles show their greatness. In thirteen games, they outscored their opponents 570–104. In the playoffs, Pine Forest set a state record by averaging forty-seven points in four victories. During the entire season, they trailed for a grand total of 1:43, which occurred against Choctawhatchee.

When asked a few days later how this team compared to some of the previous teams he coached, Madison responded, "That's hard to say. It's a mighty good one, but I hate to compare this group to others I've coached. I don't think it's fair to take one team and play it against another. But I do think you could take this team and play with anybody, anywhere in the country. I don't know what winning the national championship means, but it sure sounds good. And it will sure look good on shirts."

When the national championship became official Madison added, "Our goal from the beginning was to win state, but when we had a chance at the national championship, that became our battle cry too. It's great for us, it's great for Pensacola, and it's great for Florida. It's something nobody can ever take away from you."

For the job he did with Pine Forest, Madison received the National High School Football Coach of the Year award by *USA Today*. He had reached the pinnacle.

H.G. Bissinger's 1990 book *Friday Night Lights: A Town, a Team and a Dream*, along with the subsequent movie and television series, painted a vivid picture of the importance or even overemphasis of high school football in west Texas in the late 1980s. There were similarities in Pensacola during the entire decade, but it wasn't relegated to a single high school in a single town. Before the decade ended, there were power houses and state champions at four different schools in the area. These were the pre-internet days, and stadiums were packed on Friday nights. It wasn't unusual to have over ten thousand people at an important regular season game, and they were often on live TV. It was loud. The bands played throughout the game and put on spectacular shows at halftime. There was simply no more exciting place to be on a Friday night in Pensacola during the 1980s than at a high school football game.

Dan Shugart has been around high school football in Pensacola for over forty years. He graduated from the University of California, Los Angeles (UCLA) in 1979 and made the move to Florida in 1980 to work in radio. He has served as the sports director at WEAR television since 1982 and broadcasted high school football on WSRE for many years. Shugart's first year in Pensacola happened to coincide with Carl Madison's state championship at Tate, and he witnessed the two championships with Pine Forest. During the decade, he also saw a couple of state championships from Woodham High School and the Emmitt Smith Escambia High teams that added two of their own.

Shugart refers to the decade of the 1980s as "the Golden Age" of high school football in Pensacola. Speaking of those days, Shugart said, "Astounding how important it was and how good it was. How good the coaching was. He [Madison] and Don Sharpe [of Woodham] really more than anybody else as far as coaches, raised that level."

CHAPTER SEVEN

DECISIONS

FOLLOWING THE 1988 season, Madison made a decision that he later came to regret. At that time, he had thirty years in the Florida school system, and an offer was made to employees that should they choose to retire after their thirty years, they would receive a bonus. He decided to take the bonus and coach somewhere outside of Florida. He also made the decision based on the pension system in Florida. If he stayed another year, it would have cost him 25 percent of his pension.

He spoke of how hard it was to leave Pine Forest even with the pension situation. "Next year, Pine Forest will have fourteen starters back from a national championship team. That team can win another state championship, and no coach has ever won three straight in Florida."

Madison chose to accept both the athletic director and head football coach jobs at Westover High School in Albany, Georgia. Reactions to the announcement were predictable.

Ralph Godwin commented, "We're losing the best, and he'll be difficult to replace. But I'm not surprised he made the move. We knew Carl had several offers, and he was leaving. A man has to do what is best for his family."

Ronnie Sonnier added, "I'm sorry to see him go, and he certainly left his mark."

Madison's former defensive coordinator and Tate head coach at the time, Bobby Taylor, summed up the thoughts of many when he said, "Nobody can dispute that the Chief is a good coach and has done a lot for football in this area. He gets good mileage out of his players, and the bottom line is that he wins. It's going to be a little boring around here without him, though."

Before Madison accepted the position at Westover, he explored a number of options. His plan was to leave Florida, but he needed to think about the best location to continue coaching. A coach with the pedigree of Carl Madison enjoyed plenty of options, but he quickly determined he would either go to Texas, Alabama, or Georgia before eventually focusing on Georgia. Six schools were considered: Lowndes County, Dublin, North Cobb, Calhoun, Stockbridge, and Westover.

Madison ruled out North Cobb and Calhoun quickly for various reasons. He desired to take over a program that needed turning around. Lowndes County did not meet that criterion since they owned a winning tradition, but he still chose to interview there. During a group interview with different faculty members, administrators, the head of the quarterback club, and others, the band director asked what would happen if he didn't have an option quarterback.

Madison asked the band director in turn, "What if you don't have a drummer? I make quarterbacks."

Someone later interrupted and said, "Let me ask you this hypothetical question: how would you treat banker Jones' son and widow Smith's son?"

In a classic example of how not to answer an interview question, Madison responded in a way that indicated they would both be treated equally badly—and it did not go over well. "They're all the same to me, and if you don't hire me or Gene Cox [former Tallahassee Leon coach who found himself in the same position as Madison with the Florida retirement system], you're gonna be looking for another coach next year."

That left three schools to consider, Dublin, Stockbridge, and Westover. Dublin wanted Madison as their head football coach, but they could not provide an adequate salary. He scheduled a meeting with Stockbridge officials but cancelled it. Westover was the job he wanted, and they named him their head football coach and athletic director on February 27, 1989.

Madison did not walk into an ideal situation. The Westover football team carried a twenty-one-game losing streak and had not experienced a winning season since 1982, only managing two of them in its twenty-year history.

"Yes, I thrive on challenges. My goal is to win at Westover. I believe it can be done," Madison commented after his introduction as head coach.

Westover High school is located in Albany, Georgia in the southwestern portion of the state. It opened its doors in 1970 and for much of its history was one of four high schools to serve the population of Dougherty County. Albany High, the oldest of the four, closed in 2017. In the football-crazy state of Georgia, the Albany area has never been a particular hotbed for success. In fact, only one state championship had ever been won by a local team, Albany High in 1959.[9]

Carl Madison had three championships to his record.

Area coaches reacted to the news of Madison coming to Westover. "Oh, me, my job just got a heck of a lot tougher. I really didn't want him to take the job. It would have suited me fine if he'd stayed in Florida," said Albany's Danny Williams.

Jack Johnson of Mitchell-Baker commented, "I'll tell you one thing right now. Region 1-AAA's coaches should go to their calendars and look at next year's schedule. They need to erase that 'W' they've got circled next to Westover and replace it with a big ole question mark."

The Westover Patriots opened their 1989 season under new head coach Carl Madison against the Terrell County Greenwave. The offense had difficulty running Madison's veer, but the defense played well, holding Terrell County scoreless in a 20–0 victory. Quarterback Quincy Washington scored twice, and the twenty-one-game losing streak ended.

"Our defense played outstanding football. I was impressed with the

---

9   Dougherty County would add a second state championship in 1998.

enthusiasm it showed," Madison stated.

Mitchell-Baker came next on the schedule. In a mistake filled affair, Westover stayed close most of the way, but a couple of Mitchell-Baker touchdowns in the fourth quarter allowed the Eagles to pull away for a 28–7 victory. With the loss, Madison's own personal win streak ended at twenty-six.

Mitchell-Baker coach Johnson was somewhat gracious, in a back-handed kind of way, during his postgame comments. "Coach Madison is a great coach, but tonight we wanted to welcome him to South Georgia. This is not Florida football; this is hard-nosed South Georgia football. We wanted to show him how different football in this area is from the style of play he's used to. I'm just glad we don't play them again this year."

After a loss to Worth County, the Patriots came out with a vengeance against the Lee County Trojans, winning 77–21. Those seventy-seven points were the most points scored by a team in the Dougherty County school system since Albany High School also scored seventy-seven points in 1927.

A loss to Dougherty High School came next, and the Patriots did not play well. "They tell me it's a Westover tradition to play like we did tonight," Madison said. "This team had a total lack of pride and desire. We need people who are willing to do whatever is necessary to win. We just don't seem to have that."

Madison was never one to avoid a challenge, and he'd already proven that by taking on losing programs throughout his coaching tenure. But great coaches possess the ability to recognize early what challenges a program faces, and in some instances, they are extremely difficult to overcome. It was more difficult than he imagined it might be to go from the top of the high school football world to a place without a winning tradition and all that accompanied it.

Madison witnessed a more inspired effort from his young men when Westover defeated Thomas County-Central 22–13. But losses to Monroe, Thomasville, and the Cairo Syrupmakers followed—yes, the Syrupmakers, complete with a pitcher of syrup as a mascot.

The Patriots played Albany in their season finale. Despite their 3–6 record, Westover still maintained an opportunity to make the state play-offs as the number two seed from their subregion but needed to beat the Indians for that to happen. They trailed only 14–6 at the half and were driving for a possible tying score midway through the third quarter when Albany intercepted a pass and returned it eighty-five yards for a score. Westover never recovered, falling 40–14. Though not a great season by any stretch, three victories for a team that lost twenty-one straight coming into the campaign demonstrated significant improvement.

Not long after the finish of the season, rumors began circulating about the possibility of Carl Madison leaving Westover to return to Pensacola.

Madison didn't do much to dispel those rumors, and during the Patriots' season, he told the *Pensacola News Journal*, "I want to finish my coaching career in Florida. Pensacola's my home, and my goal is to finish coaching there."

The speculation continued into early 1990, but Madison said, "Nobody's called, and I don't know of any opening. Even if there were, they may not want me."

He went on to clarify that he couldn't make a move before summer anyway due to the structure of his retirement. Rules strictly prohibited retirees from returning to employment in the state until at least one year had passed. When Leo Carvalis stepped down at PHS in June, it seemed a foregone conclusion that Madison would take over as the new head coach.

When asked about the possibility, Madison replied, "Sounds interesting. I'm excited about it. I'm certainly going to look into it."

On Monday, July 2, 1990, Pensacola High named him their head football coach.

Madison never really wanted to leave Pensacola in the first place. The payoff from Florida retirement was just too good to pass up. When he made the decision to leave, he hoped that he could stay in Georgia long enough to begin drawing some retirement there since he spent five years at Forest Park from 1966–1971. But his home was North-west Florida for twenty-five of the past thirty years, and the draw to return was strong. Grace Madison later said that Carl's reason for leaving Westover did not involve the parents or the school and that he loved the school. He did not like the way the fundraising for the program was set up, though. He could not get it established like he wanted and believed it prevented having a high level of success. Madison also wanted to return since Grace stayed behind in Pensacola. She still needed three years in the Florida system. When an opportunity appeared, Carl Madison could not pass it up.

The headlines of the July 3 sports section of the *Pensacola News Journal* stated simply "*Heee's baaaaacckk*; PHS hires Madison." The rampant speculation proved accurate.

"I was just looking for an opportunity to come back. I've always had a deep feeling for Pensacola High. Coach [Jim] Scoggins established a great program here."

The move surprised no one. Escambia head coach Dwight Thomas commented, "We all knew that was going to happen."

Madison was excited about the team he inherited at Pensacola High. Though the Tigers only finished 4–6 the prior year, they returned fifty lettermen, including eight offensive and seven defensive starters. Quarterback Keith Harris was considered one of the top players in the area, and three offensive linemen were top college prospects.

"I've never walked into a situation where there was so much talent coming back," Madison said.

As Madison prepared for the 1990 season, *Pensacola News Journal* staff writer Scott Bihr wrote the following after a conversation with Madison:

"Is he a good guy or a bad guy? You're likely to get conflicting viewpoints depending on who you talk to.

To his friends, he is "the Chief." A dynamic, charming man whose coaching accomplishments are unparalleled.

To his foes, he is a conniving villain not worth of the lofty status mentioned above."

Madison did not deny anything, nor did he give reporters further ammunition. He deftly deflected the criticism by stating, "Whether the stories about me are true or not, they keep getting bigger and bigger. If I did everything people say, I'd be a genius."

The Pensacola High School Tigers started the season ranked number five in Florida class 4A. The number of returning lettermen contributed greatly to the high ranking, but having Madison as head coach certainly weighed significantly.

It proved an inauspicious return to Pensacola for Madison in his PHS debut when the Tigers fell 27–8 to Washington. The Tigers turned the ball over eight times.

"We just had a real poor game plan. We didn't have the continuity you have to have," Madison said, accepting much of the blame for the poor performance.

Following a week off, PHS played Pine Forest, the school Madison had led to back-to-back state championships and a national championship just two years prior. The Tigers fell to the Eagles 30–17.

Pine Forest head coach Jerry Pollard said, "I'd be lying if I said it didn't feel good. Carl and I are good friends. It feels better to beat them than to have him beat me."

Madison finally got his first victory at Pensacola High the next week when his squad defeated Bay Minette, Alabama 9–7. They followed that with another one over Tallahassee Lincoln.

The Tigers lost to Milton before beating Tate and Woodham. Then came an exciting matchup with Tallahassee Godby. It featured one of the more amazing first quarters one could ever hope to see in high school football or any level football for that matter. In a quarter that saw three touchdowns of seventy-plus yards, including Tiger Greg Walker's ninety-five-yarder, Godby led 26–20 when the clock expired. It was tied 34–34 at the half, and the Cougars led 41–34 heading into the fourth.

An Ashly Gadson score tied the score in the final quarter, and James Serwack kicked a twenty-one-yard field goal as time expired to give the Tigers a 44–41 victory.

After scoring forty-four points against Godby, the Tigers were shut out 28–0 the next week in a matchup with Choctaw. They wrapped up their season against crosstown rival Escambia in the battle for the "Ye Olde Wash Boiler" trophy. The Tigers scored twenty first-half points in a 27–15 win that put their final record at 6–4.

"I think we're a lot better than a 6–4 team. We just didn't execute when we should have. The turnovers really hurt us," Madison said.

All appeared fine for Madison at Pensacola High on the surface, but some things bothered him. The school did not have the athletic facilities he was accustomed to, or the same level of community support he'd experienced at other schools, at least in northwest Florida.

When Milton High head football coach Joel Williams resigned in February of 1991, not long before the start of spring football practice, rumors swirled that Carl Madison might return to the place he coached in the early 1960s. On March 27, all speculation ended when he accepted the job at Milton.

Madison, now fifty-nine years old, said of his return, "I've been waiting to go back to Milton for a long time. When the opportunity came up before, I couldn't take it. Milton is where I wanted to go. I thought it might never work out. It's a good, supportive football community. I remember the stands being full and good football players. I'm really looking forward to coming back."

Carl Madison returned to Milton in 1991, thirty-one years after originally taking the head coaching job there and twenty-six years after leaving for Forest Park. He believed this would be his last coaching stop given his age and the weariness of changing schools multiple times.

The Panther team Madison inherited had gone 8–4 the year prior, advancing to the sectional round of the Florida state playoffs, but only four starters returned from that group and once again he faced a challenge.

Despite their lack of experience, Milton started the season the seventh-ranked team in the Florida 4A poll. Madison expected good things from senior running back Kasai McClain, and McClain delivered in the season opener by rushing for 136 yards and three touchdowns in a 50–12 win.

The Panthers moved up to number four in the state rankings after their opening win. A week two matchup with Pensacola High School meant Madison would be coaching against kids he had coached the year before.

Heading into the contest, Madison downplayed the significance of coaching against his former team. "The game's important, but that's because it's a big district game that we'd like to win against a good football team," he said.

Things looked good for the Panthers early when they took a 6–0 lead. But the Tigers reeled off the next twenty-eight points on their way to defeating Milton 28–14.

The schedule didn't get any easier for the Panthers against Choctawhatchee. The Indians were the defending state champions, current top-ranked team in Class 5A and ranked eighth in the country by *USA Today*. In an extremely competitive contest, Elijah Williams blocked a potential game-winning field goal, and Milton secured a 35–34 victory.

"It was a very exciting game. We had a great opportunity to do something, and our people just came together and [did] it," Madison said amidst a jubilant throng of Panther supporters.

For the second week in a row, Milton faced a top-ranked team in the state. This time against 4A district rival Fort Walton Beach and their future Heisman Trophy quarterback, Danny Wuerffel. Things came back down to earth for the Panthers as they lost a hard-fought matchup 35–24. They returned to the win column the next week with an easy win against Woodham.

Victories over Niceville, Pine Forest, Escambia, and Washington moved the Panthers' record to 7–2 with just one game remaining on the schedule. They closed out their season against a 9–0 Pace team. The neighboring Patriots were a 3A squad and Milton's only matchup with a school from a smaller classification. They experienced little trouble dispatching Pace 43–15.

By most measures, it was a successful return to Milton for Carl Madison. He led his team to an 8–2 record, but it was reminiscent of his first stint with the Panthers in the 1960s when two of his undefeated squads could not participate in the state playoffs. Although Milton carried the number five ranking in the state 4A poll, only district champions advanced to the playoffs, and Fort Walton Beach earned that distinction. Danny Wuerffel and his Vikings went on to win the 1991 Florida 4A state title.

After the disappointment of having such a good season yet missing the playoffs, Madison and his Panthers entered the 1992 season determined to change their fortunes. With senior Elijah Williams and many other strong players returning, the outlook appeared bright. They ranked among the top five 4A teams in Florida heading into the campaign, and the *Pensacola News Journal* selected them the favorites for the district title.

The season opened with a convincing victory over New Orleans Clark before matching up with Pensacola High. The Tigers had handed Madison a loss the previous year, but that wasn't happening again in 1992. Williams scored three times in a 39–12 Panther victory. A 30–13 domination of Choctawhatchee followed.

Milton now ranked fourth in Class 4A while their next opponent, Fort Walton Beach, ranked third and were the defending state champions.

"They have been there before," Madison said of Fort Walton. "They have a pride in themselves and their team. They have a chance to win it [state] again."

Panther senior linebacker Joe Green added, "They're good. They think they're going to win, but deep down they know what's going to happen. If we play like we have been, we should be ok."

The contest was played at Fort Walton Beach, and the Vikings sported a 17-game winning streak. The Panthers dominated, accumulating 520 yards of total offense with Elijah Williams again carrying most of the load in a 43–13 victory that established Milton as the panhandle team to beat in Class 4A.

They had no problems with Woodham before a matchup with Niceville, the number eight ranked team in Florida 5A. The Eagles handed the Panthers their first loss in a game that had no bearing on Milton's playoff chances. Madison's squad did not waste any time the next week against Pine Forest. Jamal Collins ran fifty-five yards for a score on the second play, and Adam Ganzy later picked up a fumble and raced ninety-seven yards for a score to help the Panthers win 47–12.

A matchup with Escambia the next week provided an opportunity to clinch the district championship. The Gators had given them fits in recent history but were winless in 1992. Elijah Williams scored four times while the offense rolled up over six hundred total yards in a 62–6 dominating performance that gave them the District 1-4A title.

The final two games of the season served as preparation for the playoffs. The Panthers defeated Washington 29–0 before taking on Pace. Milton came in ranked number five in 4A while Pace sat at number two in 3A.

"It's a big game, but it's probably a little bigger for the people in Pace. We're the biggest county school, and they like to beat us," Madison said.

After a close first half, the Panthers pulled away for a 35–7 win.

In the opening round of the playoffs, Milton traveled to play a tough Tallahassee Leon team. Madison battled Leon many times in the past when Gene Cox led them, and Madison served at Tate. Now Leon was led by Coach Jim Sauls. The game proved as exciting as many of the previous Tate-Leon battles. Senior quarterback Cary Blanks ran for 294 yards and scored four times for the Panthers. Unfortunately, his Leon counterpart, Justin Whitfield, threw for five touchdowns and ran for the go-ahead score with 1:17 left to lead Leon to a 40–37 victory.

"I'm proud of our kids," Madison said. "Carey Blanks, you couldn't ask for more from him. Our offensive kids played their hearts out. But they just outplayed us. It's an end to a beautiful season."

Madison figured the 1993 season would be challenging. The team lost some of its top players, including Elijah Williams, who was now at the University of Florida, and dependable Carey Blanks. Fourteen starters in total had moved on.

Milton began the season the fifth-ranked team in Florida 4A and faced Pace in their opener. The Panthers handed the Patriots their only regular season losses the past two years with both coming in the season finales. Pace jumped out to a 17–0 lead, but Milton roared back, and when new quarterback Mike Miller scored on forty-six-yard run late, they moved in front 18–17. But on the ensuing possession, the Patriots converted a fourth and ten, and Phillip Harrellson kicked a field goal to give Pace a 20–18 victory.

Losses to Moss Point, New Orleans Edna Karr, and Tate gave the Panthers and 0–4 record to open the season. Though winless, they had yet to play within the district. Their first game of the season came in their matchup with Pine Forest.

Madison still felt his team could turn things around. "We have to eliminate our mistakes and keep our heads high. To win, you've got to hate to lose, and right now we're accepting defeat and not just going out and taking something."

"Hating to lose" was a theme Madison impressed upon his players throughout the decades he coached. He truly believed this was important. It should gnaw at you when you lost, and you should be willing to pay whatever price was necessary in preparation and during games to avoid that feeling.

The following week his Panthers did just what Madison asked of them, knocking off Pine Forest 27–12.

After defeating New Orleans Clark 55–14, things appeared back on track. Defeating district rival, Woodham, would secure a playoff berth, but then everything unraveled for Milton. In the week leading into the game, word came out that the Panthers used an ineligible player against

Pine Forest, and their victory over the Eagles was forfeited. A junior running back had forged teacher signatures on a document to illegally change a failing grade so that he could play.

Guidance counselors informed Madison of the forgery once they discovered what happened. He immediately reported it to the Florida High School Activities Association who declared their win against Pine Forest a forfeit. Milton appealed the decision and would have to wait a few weeks to find out if it would be upheld, but few felt the chances of a favorable ruling were promising.

Discussing the entire incident later, Madison said, "When I found out, it was the lowest point in my lifetime for something like that to happen."

Given the way things ended for Madison at Tate ten years earlier, it demonstrated the depth of his disappointment. The 1993 squad never recovered.

Against Woodham, it seemed the Panthers were putting the difficult news behind them. They led 13–12 with eight minutes to play. But as the team lined up to punt from their own ten-yard line, one of the players decided to call a fake. It did not work and turned out to be a critical mistake.

"Why would a kid call a fake punt? It was a punt all the way. That's what's been wrong with this team all season," Madison said.

Woodham scored shortly after the misguided attempt and won 20–13.

The Panthers dropped their final two games to Niceville and Escambia. Adding insult to injury, Milton received word a few days later that their appeal of the decision that they must forfeit their victory against Pine Forest was denied. With that, the Panthers officially concluded their 1993 season with a 1–8 record. It was a fitting ending to a miserable season, the worst of Carl Madison's career, but greater challenges of a different variety loomed.

In January of 1994, the *Pensacola News Journal* published a story that accused Madison of physically and verbally abusing players during the previous season. A group of parents filed a complaint with the Professional Practices Commission alleging wrongdoing. All parties did not agree on what occurred. A player who was reportedly kicked said that it did indeed happen, and a volunteer trainer who served in the military in the Persian Gulf and was a licensed physician's assistant discussed a number of things he believed problematic. Others who attended the season's game and practices stated that they never saw any inappropriate treatment.

Seventy-two players and coaches signed a letter penned by junior tight end Randy Ueberroth that supported Madison and denied the allegations. Madison's nephew and former quarterback at Tate, Scotti Madison, also wrote an impassioned letter published in the *Pensacola News Journal* in defense of his uncle.

Many parents and community members believed that a small group, frustrated with the team's performance of the previous season and led by a family member who had a personal disagreement with Madison, were trying to force his ousting. The superintendent of Santa Rosa County schools, Bennett C. Russell, stated that he spent "considerable time" investigating the incident and found no evidence of wrongdoing.

No one ever accused Madison of being a saint, and there are those who to this day believe the findings were incorrect. It was undeniably an extremely difficult year for him and included some of the darkest days of his life. Certainly, many people facing similar circumstances would have chosen to walk away at that point, and Madison had nothing left to prove as a football coach. His accomplishments were cemented. But he was a man who came from poverty to achieve great things, and it was not in his nature to quit when he believed he still had a lot to offer. And whether some people believed it or not, he could have a positive influence on young men.

Karl Jernigan entered his sophomore year in 1994 having only played one year of football. Baseball was his primary sport. But Madison recognized football ability in him and before that season asked him if he would like to play quarterback. Jernigan responded that he would, so the two of them worked on the skills it took to play quarterback in the Madison offense.

The quarterback holds the most important position for any offense, but in Madison's option offense, the responsibilities went well beyond the usual expectations. Reading the defense and making quick, correct decisions during the play on who got the ball was critical.

Madison later described finding the right person to play the position. "Pick somebody out and work him, and he has to understand that he is the boss out there on the field—really the game is in his hands to a certain extent—and they've got to have that pride in order to do the things it takes to win."

Carl Madison possessed the ability to find those who could run his offense effectively. He'd had Jerry Halfacre, his nephew Scotti Madison, and Keith Leonard among others at Tate; John Brown and Ronnie Sonnier at Pine Forest; over the next three years, Jernigan would add his name to that list and prove Madison's confidence in him well placed.

For the second year in a row, Milton opened against Pace. The Panthers scored on the final play of the first quarter on a run by Karl Jernigan. In the third quarter, Milton kicker Lawrence Tynes, who went on to win two Super Bowls with the New York Giants, hit a twenty-nine-yard field goal to give Milton a 9–7 lead that proved to be the final score.

The Panthers traveled to Moss Point, Mississippi the next week for the always tough matchup with the Tigers and fell 34–8. They faced another out-of-state competitor the next week in New Orleans Karr, the defending Louisiana 5A state champions and winners of fourteen straight. With less than five minutes remaining, the Panthers trailed 10–3, but Mike Miller hit Shaun Parker with a forty-two-yard touchdown pass to cut the lead to 10–9. Madison made the decision to go for two points rather than kick the point after for the tie. Marcail Hudson ran the conversion in for the score, and Milton escaped with a 11–10 victory.

An easy 27–6 win over Tate preceded a hard-fought district matchup with Pine Forest. A late tackle short of the endzone by the Milton defense allowed them to hold on for a 15–7 defeat of the Eagles.

New Orleans Clark came next on the schedule. Once again, the Panthers had no trouble with the Bulldogs, dispatching them 56–6 before playing their second district contest of the year against Woodham.

Madison commented on how completely different this Milton team was from the one a year ago. "This season there is no jealousy out there. They are all for each other," he stated.

Against Woodham, the Panthers took a 14–0 first quarter lead. The Titans scored second and third quarter touchdowns to even the score before Milton kicker Lawrence Tynes booted a twenty-seven-yard field goal with twelve seconds left in the third quarter. With less than five minutes left, Woodham retook the lead 21–17, but there was still time for the Panthers to mount a drive. With just over a minute and a half remaining, Milton faced a fourth and ten situation that they needed to convert. The play ended up going for twenty-eight yards as Jernigan completed a pass to Garrett Bagley, putting the Panthers into position at the Titan eleven-yard line. Three plays later, Jernigan hit Adam Joiner with a seven-yard touchdown pass, and Milton escaped 24–21.

"It was a great game for the players, spectators, and coaches. To come back with four minutes left showed a lot of spirit," Madison commented.

The game assured Milton of a playoff spot no matter what happened in their final district matchup with Escambia, though it would determine which team won the district championship.

Before facing off with Escambia, the Panthers had a big matchup with Niceville, the sixth-ranked team in 6A. After trailing 24–0, the Panthers rallied to within three points, but the deficit proved too much to overcome as they fell to the Eagles 24–21.

Milton faced Escambia with the district championship on the line in the final week of the regular season. They played without Karl Jernigan, who broke his thumb in practice the previous week but still managed a 35–20 victory that sent them to the playoffs.

Panama City Bay was the opponent in the first round of the 5A playoffs. Milton went to the locker room with a 9–7 lead, but Bay erupted in the second half, thanks in part to mistakes by the Panthers, to take the victory 33–17.

"We did not play a good ballgame. Our offense did not play a good game and fumbles hurt us. And our tackling was not good," a disappointed Madison said. It wasn't the ending he or any of the players envisioned to a terrific season for the program. But Milton was back.

The 1995 season presented a challenge to Milton. Washington High School, the defending 6A Florida State champions, dropped down in classification and into the same district as Milton. Other teams in the district included Woodham, Pine Forest, and Gulf Breeze. Local writers picked the Panthers to finish third in the district, behind both Washington and Woodham, though across the state they finished just outside the voting for the state top ten in 5A. Washington was voted number one.

Milton opened the season against Pace. In a defensive struggle, unusual for a Madison-coached team, the Panthers got off to a good start with a 7–0 victory. Wins over Tate, Choctaw, and two New Orleans schools ran the Panthers record to 4–0 and moved them to number four in the rankings. On Wednesday, October 3 before Milton's next contest against Pine Forest, Hurricane Opal hit the Florida panhandle area hard, and cleanup efforts forced the game to be moved back three days from its normal Friday kickoff to Monday, October 8. The Panthers had no problems with the Eagles, winning 26–0.

The change due to the hurricane meant that four days later the Panthers had to play again. Ironically, they faced New Orleans Lawless, which ten years later was devastated by Hurricane Katrina and would never reopen. Despite the brief break, Madison decided to employ a new offensive gameplan, the run and shoot. It paid dividends immediately with Milton scoring on its first three possessions. The Panthers won 35–22 to run their record to 7–0.

Milton returned to district play against Washington. The Wildcats were just 3–2 one season after winning a state championship, but Madison did not take them lightly. "We haven't played a team as good as Washington. They lost two last year, and I expect that is their battle cry again—lose two and win state again."

Marcail and Buck Hudson combined for 359 yards rushing and three touchdowns in a 31–18 victory that kept the Panthers unbeaten.

Next came Woodham, sporting a 1–1 district record. A defeat of the Panthers would put them in a tie with Milton for the district crown. Woodham was led by first year coach Mike Sherrill, who played for Madison on the 1980 Tate state championship team. For the first time in his career, Madison faced a former player on the opposing sidelines as a head coach. Milton led early 14–0, but Woodham fought back, and with thirty-seven seconds to play, the Titans completed a touchdown pass. With the extra point, Woodham led 21–20, and its fans were in a frenzy. Milton had one final chance, and after a few incomplete passes, things did not look good. With nine seconds remaining, they faced fourth down on their own thirty-six-yard line.

Karl Jernigan later described what happened next: Milton called their timeout, and he went to the sideline to speak with Madison. Madison told him to run flea flicker, flea flicker, right.

"Seriously?" Jernigan responded. They had practiced trick plays the first five minutes or so of practice all season and that play never worked. Not even in practice.

"Yes, we're going to run it, and it's going to work, and we're going to win the game," was how Madison responded according to Jernigan.

Jernigan didn't believe it would work, but he knew better than to go against the wishes of his coach. It went perfectly. Jernigan threw a short pass to Jason Shelton. Shelton tossed the ball back towards Buck Hudson at the line of scrimmage. Just before being tackled, Buck threw the ball downfield to his cousin Marcail for a touchdown.

"It was a winning play! We had that play in the game plan, and it worked out real well," a jubilant Madison said on the field as he was hugged by players and cheerleaders.

Fans in attendance would be hard pressed to come up with a stranger ending to a football game. In their high school football season wrap-up article, The *Pensacola News Journal* named the Milton-Woodham contest the best of the year in northwest Florida.

When the Panthers entered their regular season finale against Gulf Breeze, they ranked third in the Florida 5A poll. They prevailed 34–16. A remarkable thirty-one years after Madison last led Milton to an unbeaten season he did so again.

"I always thought we could do it. We were just able to work things out during the season. I am extremely proud of the kids and the coaches. I just hope we can continue to work and win some more," Madison said.

Madison led his unbeaten Panthers into the playoffs against Crestview. The Bulldogs were only 6–4, but Madison wanted to avoid any overconfidence. "Hopefully the kids realize the importance of the game because there's no second time around."

Milton trailed 16–13 after Crestview kicked a field goal on the final play of the first half. The team responded in the second half with Marcail and Buck Hudson both scoring in the third quarter to lead the Panthers to a 34–23 playoff victory. Next came Gainesville Buchholz.

Madison said of Buchholz, "They are super quick and are a pretty good football team. They have a lot of speed— more speed than anyone we have played."

Madison typically used the Bear Bryant approach of overhyping his opponents. Just as he learned the veer offense from Bill Yeoman, he took this mental approach from The Bear. Despite his public comments, he certainly expected his unbeaten Panthers to prevail given that the Bobcats had four losses on the season.

Milton played well early. When halftime arrived, they had a double-digit lead and felt confident. But things changed dramatically in the second half. The Panthers couldn't stop the Bobcat offense, led by Doug Johnson, who later went on to star at the University of Florida and spend seven years in the NFL. When Buchholz scored with under two minutes remaining, the Panthers trailed 35–34. Jernigan led Milton on a drive and with some time still remaining, they moved into range for a game winning Tynes field goal. But while trying to get in better position for the final kick, they suffered a fumble that ended their chances. It was an extremely difficult season-ending loss, and Madison would later remember it among the most bitter.

The Milton Panthers had Karl Jernigan returning for his third season as the team's starting quarterback in 1996. Madison called Jernigan "a true student of the game, a special football player."

"He's our leader, no question about it," said offensive lineman Cody Quillion.

The extreme disappointment of having one of his better teams upset in the playoffs the year before wasn't something Carl Madison would dwell on. With a new season came renewed hope. Madison believed it was the fastest team he'd coached to that point, high praise considering his dominant Pine Forest teams in the late 1980s.

The Panthers entered their season opener with Pace on a twelve-game regular season unbeaten streak and ranked number three in the 5A poll.

"Apparently, the ranking is based on the success we had last year. We are proud of it, but we would like to be number one at the end of the year. It's where you end up that counts," Madison said.

Milton got off to a quick start with a 38–8 victory.

The Panthers moved to number two in the 5A poll by the time they met Tate. Milton ran its regular season win streak to thirteen with a 41–8 defeat of Tate when five Panther players scored, and the defense forced five turnovers.

The tenth-ranked 6A Choctawhatchee Indians came next on the schedule. Leading into the matchup that week, Madison made it clear that although he was pleased with the play of his starters, the performance of the backups was unacceptable.

"This week they must play better, or they're gone," he stated.

Unfortunately, the second string did not see much of the field against the Indians. Choctaw's offense outgained the Panthers by almost 150 yards and blew out the Panthers 45–12.

Victories over Perry Walker, New Orleans Clark, and Pine Forest improved their record to 5–1. Milton was on a roll and didn't appear to need anything, but they got an addition the next week when Marcail

Hudson became eligible to play for the first time since his suspension at the beginning of the season for off-the-field troubles. Hudson made up for lost time by rushing for over one hundred yards, returning two punts for more than thirty yards each, and intercepting a pass in a 63–0 defeat of New Orleans Lawless.

Washington, with a record of 1–5, did not appear to present a threat to the Panthers but played much better than anyone expected. When the Wildcats intercepted a last minute pass on their own one-yard line, it went to overtime. After both teams traded touchdowns in the first overtime, Milton kicked a field goal on their possession in the second overtime period. Facing fourth and goal from the five-yard line and trailing 31–28, Washington coach Chet Bergalowski decided to go for the win. When Wildcat quarterback Demarion McCants kept on the option and worked his way into the endzone, Washington secured an improbable upset.

"This was a big one. I am sure Mr. Robinson is pleased," Bergalowski said while speaking of former Washington coach Sherman Robinson, for whom the Wildcats' new stadium had been named. The victory over the Panthers was their first in the stadium.

Milton took out their frustrations the next couple of weeks, 50–20 over Woodham and 42–9 over Gulf Breeze in the season finale.

Advancing to the playoffs set up a trip to Fort Walton Beach to take on the defending state champions Vikings. Jernigan returned from a shoulder injury against Gulf Breeze, but the Hudson cousins put on a show once again. Buck ran for four scores, and Marcail gained 242 yards in the 41–21 Panther victory. Next came Jacksonville Parker, who had defeated top-ranked Ocala Vanguard to make it to the second round.

Madison shared his thoughts leading into the matchup. "We probably played our best game of the season against Fort Walton Beach. This week, hopefully we can get after it early and stay with it. They are bigger than we are and have pretty good speed."

Milton found themselves trailing 14–13 with less than five minutes to play before Buck Hudson broke up the middle and ran thirty-three yards for the go ahead score. The Panthers held on and advanced to the third round of the playoffs against Lakeland.

The high-powered Milton offense could never get things going against Lakeland, and the Dreadnaughts prevailed 13–0. Two turnovers in the second half hurt the Panthers.

"It was very disappointing. I'd like to play them again because we've got a better club than we showed tonight. But we just didn't come up with the plays," said Madison. For Karl Jernigan, it was his last football game. He chose the baseball route in college, playing for Florida State and being a big part of College World Series teams there. He completed his Milton career with a 32–5 record as the starting quarterback.

The Fellowship of Christian Athletes Challenger Awards banquet has been held in Pensacola every year on the first Monday of December since 1968. All the northwest Florida football teams and their coaches gather together for dinner to hear a keynote speech from a successful sports figure who highlights their own faith. Speakers over the years included Dallas Cowboys coach Tom Landry, NFL Hall of Famer Gale Sayers, NFL great Rosie Grier, Florida State coach Bobby Bowden, Baylor University coach Grant Teaff, and New York Yankee great Bobby Richardson. At the banquet one young man from each team is presented an award, voted on by his teammates, for the person who best represents Christian values, sportsmanship, and academic achievement.

Mike Killam, a star lineman for Madison at Tate who went on to Auburn, has been with the Fellowship of Christian Athletes (FCA) for thirty years and a Region Development Director for the past thirteen. He has maintained a close relationship with Madison since his playing days in the 1970s and spent countless days praying for his former coach. Madison always attended the Challenger Awards banquet while coaching in the area—as all head coaches did—but to Killam it seemed perfunctory. Madison always insisted his entire team attend, but it was more for them than for him. He wasn't hostile to Christianity. In fact, he spoke openly about how what a great group of Christian boys his 1980 Tate state championship team had been. It just never appeared to personally interest him.

At the 1997 banquet, former University of Florida head basketball coach John Lotz gave the speech. Killam recalls the speech being good but not necessarily one that stood out among the best over the years, though it certainly resonated with some of the attendees.

Cards at the guest tables read, "Tonight, I asked Christ to come into my heart" with a box to check if the person had done so. Contact information was also included, so someone from the FCA could follow up. After the event, it stunned Killam to see that one of the cards with a checked box had Carl Madison's name.

He called Madison the next morning to ask if he had indeed checked the box.

After a brief pause that seemed like an eternity, Madison replied, "Yes, I did. That's alright isn't it?"

A much relieved and thrilled Killam told him that it was quite alright. Speaking further on the Christian belief of eternity in heaven, Killam went on to add, "You know you're going to live forever now, right?"

Madison responded, "Well I've got a lot to learn."

Killam then thought about how he could best help his former coach begin to learn more and suggested they meet at least every other week for a while to go through the book of John, which Madison agreed to do.

A few months later at the Florida High School Coaches Convention, Killam reserved a spot at his table for Madison at the FCA prayer breakfast. The other guests at the table were stunned when Killam told them that Madison was joining them. As the program began, Madison was nowhere to be found, but he showed up just a few minutes later and took his spot at the table. He stayed long after the end of the breakfast, talking to his fellow coaches and even drawing up plays on napkins. They were convinced of his sincerity.

It wouldn't be accurate to say that Carl Madison underwent a complete change or that those who knew him no longer recognized the man he once was. Madison remained fiery and intense on the football field, and his competitive nature was not diminished in any way. But it is difficult to question what is going on inside a person and know their thoughts. To question another person's religious experience is the height of arrogance.

What can be said is that Madison had never been one to darken the doors of any of the local churches before, and after the FCA breakfast, things soon changed. He and Grace found a home in Pensacola at a local church and attended regularly. In the years since, Killam has invited Madison to numerous FCA events in the area, and he has almost always attended.

After taking his Milton Panther's deeper in the playoffs than they had been in many years in 1996, Madison looked forward to the 1997 season. Before the season, Madison commented regarding his squad, "We have three players who are 4.0 [GPA] students, and a bunch that are 3.4 or 3.5. But football intelligence, that's a big difference. Whether or not we have football intelligence, we'll see."

The season opener once again took place against Pace. It was an extremely sloppy one with thirteen fumbles between the two teams, seven by the Patriots and six by the Panthers. Duane Corlett, a transfer from Pace, played quarterback against his former teammates because Eric Cabaniss broke his collarbone on the first day of practice in pads. Corlett was the difference in Milton's 21–7 win, rushing for 103 yards, including a forty-eight-yard touchdown.

A loss to Fort Walton Beach preceded victories over New Orleans Clark and New Orleans Lawless. Then came time for Escambia.

Madison downplayed his team's chances. "We're respectable, but we can't match up with [Escambia's personnel]. They're faster and bigger than we are."

The Panthers fell behind early on a bizarre play when they fumbled at the Gator fifteen-yard line, and Escambia lateraled the ball twice on their way to an eighty-five-yard touchdown return. They led the entire way. Milton had an opportunity to tie late, but Greg Allen Jr. was stopped on the potential game-tying two-point conversion, and the Panthers fell 28–26.

Milton defeated Pine Forest and Washington before taking on Woodham. Seniors on the Titan team vividly recalled their last second flea flicker loss to the Panthers two years prior.

T.J. Davis was on the field when it happened. "The tears just started falling. That was a hard-fought game. It was a very tough loss," he said as his team prepared for their matchup with Milton.

Woodham controlled things most of the way, but the Panthers scored sixteen points in the fourth quarter to tie the score 23–23. But this time a late touchdown from Woodham made the difference as the Titans defeated the Panthers 30–23, giving Milton its second district loss and severely damaging their playoff hopes.

Milton lost again the next week to Mike Bennett's Pensacola High squad. Despite the loss, Milton went into its season finale with Gulf Breeze with an opportunity to make the playoffs. In a thrilling game against the Dolphins, Milton trailed 24–20 in the fourth quarter before Duane Corlett raced forty-four yards, and the Panthers escaped 28–24. Combined with Woodham's victory over Escambia, that put them in the state playoffs as district runner-up. Unfortunately, they would have to face the number one team in the state, Panama City Rutherford at Panama City in their playoff opener.

The Rutherford Rams had not allowed a team within fourteen points of defeating them all season, and Madison knew it would be a challenge. The Panthers gained over three hundred yards on offense and managed leads of 7–0 and 14–7 in the first half, but Rutherford scored the final thirty-five points to win 42–14 and end Milton's season.

James Broxson was a sophomore on the 1998 squad. His father Mickey was a star for Carl Madison's first Milton teams in the early 1960s. With James suiting up for the Panthers, he and Mickey became the first father-son combination to play for Madison. The Broxsons still lived in Holley, Florida, but by the time James entered high school, there was a school closer than Milton, Navarre High. Mickey applied for and received a special exemption to allow James to attend Milton. He wanted his son to play football for Carl Madison.

In the summer following James' eighth-grade year, Madison talked Mickey into allowing him to attend "camp" with the team for a week at Camp Koinonia. It was an opportunity for James to bond with members of the team, and there was a creek for swimming. It sounded fun. But he had no idea what he was getting into. Other than a daily chapel service and the occasional brief swim in the creek, "camp" turned out to consist of four-a-day practices—before breakfast, before lunch, before dinner, and again after dinner. The team referred to the site not as Camp Koinonia, but "Hell's half acre."

James had never been so homesick in his life. But he survived.

First-year quarterback, junior Keith Cone, looked sharp in the opener against Pace. He ran for seventy-two yards and passed for seventy-four as the Panthers prevailed 30–17. Pace fumbled nine times with the Panther defense recovering two of the nine. "Overall, I was satisfied with what I saw. We made some mistakes to work on, but it's always good when you can win your opener," Madison said.

The defense played much better in their second game of the season, but Milton found itself in a scoreless tie at the half against Fort Walton Beach. Things improved in the second half with Greg Allen, Jr. running for two touchdowns while the Panthers went on to defeat the Vikings 19–7.

The annual matchups with New Orleans-area schools came next, and once again, Milton had no problem winning either one and moved up to number seven in the poll ahead of their first big test against Escambia, also unbeaten. It would go a long way towards deciding the district championship.

"Whoever wins this game is in the driver's seat in the district, but if you don't win, it's not the end of the world. It'll be hard for one team to win this district without a loss. I'm just anxious to see how we stack up," Escambia coach Ronnie Gilliland said.

Things looked good early when Milton defender William Jackson stripped the ball from the Gators and ran it in for the score. Milton later took a 14–0 lead but couldn't hold on, falling 24–17.

As all great coaches do, Madison blamed himself for a trick play that backfired and allowed the Gators to score late in the first half to tie the score. "That was a stupid mistake I made before the half on that trick play. It was a terrible coaching mistake."

Milton dropped their next two contests to Pine Forest and Washington, eliminating the Panthers from the playoffs. It is difficult for a team to play when the goals they set for themselves are no longer attainable. The Panthers found themselves in just such a situation when they faced Woodham, the defending district champions and currently unbeaten in district play. They responded well in a 17–14 upset of the Titans, but a 27–14 loss to Pensacola High the next week dropped their record to 5–4. The Panthers managed to secure a winning season by defeating Gulf Breeze in their final game.

Of his 1998 Milton squad, Madison said, "We had the size but didn't have the intensity to be good football players. Our kids were fine young men, polite and all, but when you put that uniform on your personality has to change, and I don't think their personalities changed to become aggressive."

Coming off consecutive 6–4 seasons, Madison looked forward to the 1999 campaign. Others might have thought he needed to prove he still had it, that the game had not passed him by, but Madison stopped feeling like he needed to prove anything long ago. That might have been the case in Atmore as a poor kid living away from his parents, but it certainly wasn't the case now.

Classification shuffle and district lineup changes found Milton as a 3A school in a district with Pace, Gulf Breeze, and Quincy Shanks in 1999.

"We'll have a little more speed than we had, and that helps a lot. The line's a lot smaller, and we'll have linemen at 215 [pounds], 220, 225—somewhere in that range. We have a group that's gung ho and wants to play. So far, it's been a pleasure," he told the *Pensacola News Journal*.

The Panthers fell in overtime in the opener with Pine Forest but responded with a 26–20 win over a strong New Orleans West Jefferson team. Convincing victories over Lucedale, Mississippi; New Orleans

Clark, and Gulf Breeze pushed Milton's record to 4–1 going into their matchup with Escambia. It was tied 14–14 until the fourth quarter when Gator quarterback Brett Gilliland hit Adrian Walker with a touchdown pass. A later field goal made the final 24–14 Escambia.

Grace Madison met her husband on the field as reporters interviewed him. "I'm sorry, honey," she told him.

"I know," Madison responded. "It sure is hard for us to beat this team, ain't it baby."

A district matchup with Quincy Shanks High came next. The victor was all but assured of obtaining one of the two district playoff spots at the end of the regular season, and the Panthers dominated Shanks 66–22.

The Panthers had already clinched a playoff berth when they stepped up in class to take on Woodham. Madison secured his 299th win as a head coach with a 21–7 victory. He would have an opportunity to get his 300th win the next week against the Pace Patriots and secure the district title in the process.

Coming in, Milton had defeated Pace seventeen of nineteen times, including the last five. Most of those came against far less talented Patriot teams. This Pace team was 8–0 and ranked number three in 3A. It was the first time the two teams ever faced off as members of the same district. Pace raced out to a 21–0 halftime lead on their way to a 21–14 win, denying Madison his 300th victory.

He got another shot against Pensacola High School with their head coach and Madison's former player, Mike Bennett. Pensacola High School running back Jermaine Richardson rushed for 356 yards the previous week against Crestview. If Madison was going to get number three hundred, his Milton team would need to slow down Richardson. The Panthers would not be denied. Myron Franklin ran for 167 yards, and Jared Andrews scored twice in a 28–6 Milton victory. The Milton defense held Richardson to just sixty-three rushing yards. Madison's 300th win placed him among the elite high school football coaches in the country.

"I hate losing to him, and he knows it," Bennett said. "I love the guy, and he's been a father figure to me, but I can't stand losing to him. I want him to win the state championship more than I wanted him to get his 300th win."

Madison minimized the importance of the achievement. "I didn't care about the three hundredth. The winning is the most important thing, whether it's number one, five, or three hundred."

By virtue of finishing as the runner-up in their district, Milton made the state 3A playoffs and with that came a date with the third-ranked team in the state, 10–0 Palatka. The Panthers played well at Palatka, but it appeared their efforts would fall short when they trailed 14–7 with less than three minutes remaining. Then Panther defender Ray Jackson returned a blocked punt thirty-two yards for a touchdown, sending it into overtime. Palatka scored first in the overtime, but their kicker, who hadn't missed an extra point the entire season, failed on his attempt. When Milton answered with a score on a one-yard run by Keith Cone and Tim Baxley added the extra point, the Panthers escaped with a thrilling 21–20 upset.

A second-round matchup with Santa Fe Alachua came next for the Panthers. Santa Fe led 28–20 midway through the fourth quarter. Milton scored, but Keith Cone was stopped short of the goal on the two-point conversion, and Milton's season ended with a 28–26 loss.

It proved to be the last game Madison ever coached at Milton High School. On the opening day of Spring football practice for the 2000 season, first-year principal Lewis Lynn informed Madison that he would no longer be coaching the Panthers.

The school released a statement following the dismissal—"We appreciate Coach Madison's years of service to Milton High School"—but offered no explanation for his termination.

Lynn commented, "There wasn't one reason I would single out. He has had a lot of success, and he's done a good job in the past. My decision was what was best for the future."

Madison planned to retire. "I won't be coaching," he said at the time. "I've really had enough of it. I enjoyed it. I've had great people to work with. It's time. My wife [Grace] has been wanting me to."

Reaction from the coaching community came swiftly. Mike Bennett said there wasn't a better teacher "on the face of the earth. There were times I didn't like him. Especially when it's over, you want to ring his neck. Now twenty years later, I look back and everything the guy told you is right. He made me a better person, a better coach. He's the reason I'm coaching today. [Madison not coaching] is probably a tragedy for football in this area. He's only the second-winningest coach in the state of Florida. In my opinion, you couldn't get a finer football coach."

James Broxson, who would no longer get to play his senior season under Madison commented, "He didn't just teach you about the game. He teaches you about life."

Broxson would later say that he wished he could have said what he really thought about Madison's dismissal at the time, but it would not have been printable. His mother originally didn't want him to play for Carl Madison. She heard the stories about Madison and just didn't feel she wanted James around him. But the years of watching her son play for Madison completely changed her opinion, and she was as upset as anyone when Madison was let go. She called everyone she could, including the superintendent of schools, to voice her extreme displeasure, and she pulled no punches.

Madison reflected on his career shortly after the firing. "I've never had a player say he was sorry he played for me. I've had a lot come up wishing they hadn't quit. All of them say about me [that] they were treated right. They worked hard, but they were treated fair. No favorites. . . . The change that came about in the players, the school, the community, that change, you feel it. I've enjoyed that type of thing. I wouldn't change nothing. It's been a thrill."

It appeared Carl Madison's coaching days were over. He had a great run, amassing a record of 301-130-7, three state championships, and one national championship. He would be remembered as one of the great coaches, not only in Florida High School history but around the nation. Who could have believed at the time that one of his greatest coaching accomplishments was yet to come?

CHAPTER EIGHT

FINAL GLORY

O F ALL THE accomplishments Carl Madison achieved in his illustrious coaching career, what he did at Jackson Academy may very well be the most impressive.

Jackson Academy is a small private school in the Alabama Independent School Association (AISA) located in Jackson, in the southwestern part of the state. The school opened in the late 1950s and originally offered just grades one through six. A junior high and high school were added later, and the first football team took the field in 1962. Over the years, the Eagles achieved limited success and in 2002, after losing all its games the previous season while sporting an overall losing streak of fourteen, Jackson Academy needed a new football coach.

Paul Parham was a local businessman involved in the founding of Jackson Academy and the chairman of the board of the school for twenty-five years. He had three children graduate from the school. Parham served on the search committee for the football coach in 2002 and was present for Carl Madison's interview. Parham recalled his first impression of Madison as just an old man—although Parham and Madison were approximately the same age—and thought Madison was probably no longer up to the challenge of coaching high school boys.

Parham and the rest of the committee decided to go in a different direction and made an offer to another coach who accepted the position. That coach later backed out. With the season fast approaching, they had to do something quickly. Parham called a friend who had coached baseball at Auburn and knew Madison. He asked him for his thoughts. His friend told him if there was any way to get Madison, they needed to do it.

By then, Madison wasn't even sure he wanted the job and decided to make demands so unrealistic that they would have no choice but to drop their offer. He told the committee he wouldn't answer to anyone regarding football decisions, and that he would not teach any classes at the school.

"He came in and told us exactly what he was going to do, instead of us telling him what we wanted him to do," Parham stated. If he thought that would be enough to dissuade them, he was mistaken. "He didn't know how desperate we were," Parham added.

They offered the position to Madison, he accepted it, and two weeks prior to the season opener, he showed up to meet his team.

It is worth noting that in his almost fifty years of coaching football at numerous schools, Madison never coached in an affluent area. Sons of doctors, lawyers, and businessmen played for him, but he primarily coached young men from blue-collar families. His own upbringing and desire to help boys from similar circumstances certainly played a part in things working out that way, whether he gave it much thought or not. The fact that hard-working families were less likely to try to interfere and let him do his job the way he believed he needed to do it probably played a role as well.

Carl Madison became the fourth head football coach in four years for Jackson Academy, and there was weariness in the program from the constant change but also hope. An article from the August 8, 2002 edition of *The South Alabamian* had the title, "Former coach of National High School Champions heads JA football program." The community also felt optimistic because the team had moved down a class from 2A to 1A and would play against schools of similar size.

Madison inherited a group with only four returning seniors, nine juniors, and nine new players. Still, he believed he had something to work with. "We've got a chance to have a pretty good little team if we can find a lineman or two. Our main thing at the beginning of the season is to bring this group of young men together to become a family," he stated.

At his age and with his experience, he still recognized what seems so simple but is often overlooked by many coaches; for a team to be able to work together towards success, they should genuinely care about one another.

When they began preparing for the fall season, they went to a place they called "Headquarters" for two-a-day practices. The location was basically a cow pasture, and they stayed overnight so they could wake up each morning and get back to work. The practices went from sunrise to sunset. Madison immediately commanded respect, and everyone recognized a culture change.

The 2002 Jackson Academy Eagles opened their season at Lakeside Academy in Eufala. The Eagles trailed 7–6 at the half. In the second half, quarterback John Ryan Colvin hit Paul Howard for a touchdown pass, but the two-point conversion failed, and Carl Madison's Jackson Academy team lost their first game 14–12.

Colvin recalled the long, rainy four-hour bus ride home after the loss. He felt the Eagles should have won and was extremely disappointed. A 40–7 loss to Choctaw Academy ran Jackson Academy's losing streak to sixteen. At that point, everyone involved with the program needed something good to happen.

Travis Overstreet was a sophomore at the time, and like most of the boys of his class, served as a backup in 2002. He recalled some of the kids complaining early on about the length of the practices under Madison. They were not accustomed to three hours or longer on the practice field in the sweltering south Alabama sun. But Overstreet and others soon noticed that every day while he and the other boys headed home, Madison sat in his office studying the film of upcoming opponents. They realized that he was putting in more time than they were, and that made an impression.

There were certainly things one could question about the man and his coaching style throughout his career, but work ethic was not one of them. It could be argued that his work ethic had the most lasting impact on those who played for him over the years. When their playing days were over and they entered the real world, the challenges of hard work were not new to them. Battling adversity and maintaining focus weren't new either. Carl Madison had prepared them for that and a lot more on a daily basis.

Week three provided an opportunity for the Eagles against Autauga Academy. When they raced out to a 23–6 halftime lead, they began to believe that it might be their night. Any chance of getting comfortable disappeared in the second half when Autauga Academy scored two touchdowns and cut the margin to 23–22 with just over seven minutes remaining. The Eagle defense stepped up in the final minutes when Nick Evans recovered a fumble for a score, and Caleb Adley intercepted a pass with under a minute to play. Finally, Jackson Academy ended their long losing streak 29–22.

Travis Overstreet recalled walking off the field thinking, *Wow. We won.*

It had been almost two years since any Jackson Academy player tasted victory, and the team felt both joy and relief. Madison and the Eagles were just getting started.

Early during the 2002 football season, Jackson Academy held a powder puff football game in which girls from the school played while boys handled the cheerleading duties. The cheerleaders included Justin Dailey, Cody Andrews, Wesley Arnold, John Steele, Kirby Hoven, and Clay Walker. The group went all out for their cheerleading routine, and their spirit and sense of humor caught the attention of Madison. Within a couple of weeks, Madison approached the boys after finding some old school band uniforms from the 1970s. They had been packed away in a campus closet after the band had folded due to lack of student interest. They were preserved in bags from a local dry cleaner and remained in very good shape. Madison gave the boys the uniforms and asked them to do something at one of the games. They proceeded to purchase cheap instruments including a kazoo, plastic drum set, and a tambourine along with other items and thus was the beginning of what came to be known as "The Hundred Dollar Band."

Their first performance occurred at home and was a hit. So they continued. In addition to performing at home, they took their show on the road for some important contests. They informed the host schools they had a band who would like to perform at halftime. No practices or rehearsals occurred. They didn't even play real songs, mostly just made noises with the instruments and were, for all intents and purposes, completely impromptu.

The band wasn't as popular on the road as at home where the Jackson Academy fans were in on the joke. In fact, they worked in some taunting of the opposing team into their "routines" for good measure. Justin Dailey said years later that fans from their local rival Clarke Prep wanted to fight them when their performance delayed the start of their halftime homecoming activities. At the state championship game at Troy University, the Hundred Dollar Band did not receive a warm reception and caused some controversy. But none of that bothered them nor did it bother Carl Madison. He enjoyed seeing people at his schools get excited about the football program and want to contribute in some way.

After finally earning a victory, Jackson Academy added a second one when they steamrolled Ashford Academy 43–6. In their fifth game of the season, the Eagles took on Greenville Academy. Madison's team won its third in a row, rolling up 347 yards of total offense while the defense surrendered just 133 yards to the Tornadoes. A 47–6 defeat of Demopolis Academy ran their record to 4–2.

Against Abbeville Christian Academy, Casey Dyson ran for a fifty-six-yard score on the first play from scrimmage as the Eagles raced out to a 21–0 halftime lead on their way to a 27–14 win, but the next contest against South Montgomery Christian provided more of a challenge.

South Montgomery Christian, the number one team in the East

Region, traveled to Jackson to take on the Eagles. The Eagles fell behind early 6–0, but John Ryan Colvin's touchdown and the ensuing point after began a first half explosion by Jackson Academy. With touchdowns by Casey Dyson, Clay Carpenter, David Castle, and another one by Colvin, the Eagles led 33–6 at halftime. SMCA proved they were not going to surrender their number one spot without a fight in the second half when they cut the lead to 33–26, but Madison's squad responded with the final two scores on their way to a 43–26 victory.

Jackson Academy could clinch the East Region championship the next week against Sparta Academy and along with it a host spot for their first playoff game. There was no denying the Eagles. The offense rolled up 499 total yards in a 53–22 thrashing of Sparta.

The regular season finale held no playoff implications, but it offered an opportunity for Clarke County bragging rights against Clarke Prep. The Gators were in a higher classification, and Jackson Academy could not match up with them, losing 37–0 and ending their seven-game winning streak.

"Clarke Prep was just out of our class. They were bigger, faster, and better than we were. We didn't play very well either," Madison said. "The state championship game will be at Troy State on November 22. That's our goal."

Jackson Academy Athletic Director Steve Lowery, whose father Bill played for Madison at Ernest Ward, commented on Madison during his first season at Jackson Academy. "As far as I'm concerned, he's the best high school coach in the country. When we had an opportunity to get him here, I knew what he could do for the kids and the school." Lowery also said, "At first over the summer, [the team's] goal was just to win one game. Now, they want to win a state championship. That comes from the confidence the coach has in them. The kids believe they can win now."

The change that Madison created with the team, the school, and the community cannot be overstated. It was truly remarkable, and Lowery's comments give one a sense of what the man meant to everyone associated with Jackson Academy.

The first step towards a state championship came against Warrior Academy in round one of the playoffs. At the half, the Eagles led only 13–7, but third quarter touchdowns by Carpenter and Dyson put things away, and Jackson Academy advanced.

Next came Shelby Academy. "They are pretty fast, and they have a couple of pretty good size players. Our advantage will be that we are playing at home," Madison stated.

A victory would send Jackson Academy to the state championship game. Shelby Academy scored on their first possession to take a 6–0 lead, but the Eagles responded quickly with a Casey Dyson score. In the second quarter, Shelby regained the lead 12–7. Jackson Academy responded again on a Colvin to Nick Evans scoring pass to grab a 14–12 lead. With only twenty-three seconds left in the half, Colvin threw another touchdown strike, this time to Paul Howard, making the score 21–12. Two fourth quarter scores by the Eagles provided a final margin of 35–12. Jackson Academy headed to Troy for a state championship date.

Jackson Academy faced a rematch with South Montgomery Christian Academy in the championship. "If we do the right things and do them often enough, we'll be alright against South Montgomery Friday," Madison said.

By kickoff, memories of a winless 2001 season were long gone. The Jackson Academy squad was a confident one. After kicking off to the Generals, the Eagles forced an early fumble, and in less than a minute and a half, John Ryan Colvin scored. Colvin added another score a few minutes later, and David Castle ran for one to increase the lead to 22–0 by the end of the first quarter. Much like the first contest between the two, the Generals did not quit. After scoring two of the next three touchdowns, South Montgomery trailed only 28–16. But they never got any closer. All the remaining scoring came from the Eagles.

While Jackson Academy piled on the points, Travis Overstreet suggested to one of his fellow sophomore teammates, "If we score one more touchdown, we're going to get to play in the state championship game!"

The Eagles did score again, and Overstreet and other backup players got to experience the thrill of playing. When the final whistle blew, the score was 54–16. Madison had orchestrated the greatest single-season turnaround of his career. The Eagles, winless in 2001, were AISA 1A state champions in 2002.

"Come on back, and we'll do it again next year," Madison said.

Years later, John Ryan Colvin said of going from winless the previous year to a state championship the next, "Living in the area we lived in, high school football was everything. You measure your success, you measure your self-worth, you measure your identity . . . on how well you do in football. That may not be healthy in a lot of ways, but that's the way that it is in the culture we grew up in. Going from 0–10 to winning a state championship changed so many things about the way that guys on the team viewed themselves, the way the community saw the school, and even the way other schools and communities saw Jackson as a whole. I could see the morale in the school change from one year to the next. People in the school started picking up trash. People started taking pride in keeping the bathrooms clean. Same with the cafeteria."

"People wanted to give back because they knew they were a part of something they could be proud of. It's one thing to come in and change a lot of policies and practices, but it's another to change the entire culture of a school and a team. It's more valuable than anything that can be purchased. I don't know if Coach Madison fully realized how profound an impact he had on so many people. It really can't be measured."

Following the amazing 2002 season, the expectations were high for the Jackson Academy Eagles of 2003. Several key players returned including John Ryan Colvin, Lee Evans, Johnny Nichols, Cody Ready, David Castle, Clay Carpenter, and Travis Overstreet.

John Ryan Colvin had attended Jackson Academy for all of his school years and now began his senior year as quarterback for the Eagles. His father, Bill, who often attended practices, noticed the efficiency of Madison's practices. They didn't spend time strictly on conditioning but worked it into every drill. It struck him how Madison stressed perfection in exactly how you blocked, the steps the quarterback took, the way to handoff, etc. He had not witnessed anything like it at Jackson Academy until Madison arrived.

The season began against a Lakeside team that Madison predicted would be tough, but they didn't prove as formidable as expected. After giving up an opening drive touchdown, the Eagles scored the final forty-seven points in a 47–6 dominating performance.

The Eagles went on the road for the first time in the 2003 season to face South Choctaw Academy, the number one ranked team in the state. They escaped with a well-earned 19–7 victory. Convincing wins over Autauga, Ashford, and West Alabama Prep ran the Eagles record to 5–0. Late against West Alabama Prep while Madison played most of his reserves, he directed the quarterback to take a knee.

Over the loudspeaker, the announcer for West Alabama said, "Jackson Academy is showing a lot of class."

During a timeout, the reserve players pleaded with Madison to allow them to try to score since they didn't get many opportunities to do so. When the Eagles ran some plays and scored again, the announcer came on to say, "I take back what I said."

On the way to Abbeville, the team bus travelled through Troy, Alabama, the site of their state championship the year before and where it would be played again in 2003. Madison directed the bus driver to pull over near the football stadium. He had the players exit the bus and enter the stadium so they could walk around on the field. Madison made it clear that this was where they wanted to be in a few weeks, celebrating back-to-back state titles.

Jackson Academy did not particularly look like a team that would be playing for the state championship in a few weeks when they struggled in the first half against the Abbeville Christian Generals. They trailed 8–7 when the two teams headed to the halftime locker rooms. But the Eagles got it going in the second half when David Castle scored for the second time to give Jackson Academy the lead in the third quarter, and they eventually coasted to a 37–8 win.

The Eagles took a 6–0 record into their matchup against another

Generals squad, this time from South Montgomery Academy, their opponents in the 2002 State Championship. Jackson Academy scored the final thirty points to win 52–22. A 61–0 thrashing of Sparta Academy led into a matchup with Clarke Prep, the last team to defeat the Eagles. Although it made no difference in their playoff prospects, the Eagles wanted nothing more to finish the regular season undefeated by beating their county rivals. Jackson Academy found themselves trailing 12–7 with less than nine minutes left before Lee Evans took a John Ryan Colvin pitch and raced eighty yards for the go ahead score. Late in the game, Clay Carpenter added a twenty-eight-yard scoring run, and the Eagles completed their perfect regular season with a 22–12 victory. It was a big win and an important one for the school, one that also gave them momentum heading into the playoffs where the Eagles would attempt to defend their state title.

The Eagles matched up with West Alabama Academy in the first round of the playoffs, a team they defeated 54–0 earlier in the season. They started slowly but found their stride and advanced 40–7.

In the semifinals, Jackson Academy had another rematch, this time with South Montgomery Academy. David Castle returned the opening kickoff ninety-seven yards for a touchdown, and the Eagles cruised 62–7. They were on to the state championship game and an opportunity to win back-to-back titles.

Jackson Academy faced a tough Shelby Academy squad in the championship game. The Raiders were 11–1, and their only loss came at the hands of a 3A school, Bessemer. The Eagles turned the ball over six times in the first half on four fumbles and two interceptions, a performance that would crush most teams. Yet, incredibly, they led 22–8 at the break. On their first offensive play of the second half, David Castle raced forty-nine yards for a score, and the Eagles knew the championship was theirs for the taking. John Ryan Colvin scored a final touchdown to cap his high school playing days, and the Eagles won 42–8. Jackson Academy had their second straight state championship, and this time it came in an unbeaten season.

Madison commented, "It's been a good run. This has been a great group of kids to work with. They have so much character, and they believe in themselves. The first title meant a lot because the team had been so down. This one means a lot, too because we defended the title."

Grace Madison reflected later on Carl making the move to Jackson Academy. "They weren't thinking state championship [when they hired him]. They just wanted to win some games."

Not long after the championship concluded, the speculation began on whether it was Carl Madison's final game. Most assumed so, although Madison had yet to make up his mind. He later said that on the field following the championship, he felt like he was probably finished, but he spent time thinking and discussing it with his wife Grace.

Finally, at the football banquet the next week, he addressed the crowd of players, parents, and supporters. "We're coming back!" he announced.

The crowd stood applauding and shouting their approval. It was an extremely popular decision.

Assistant coach Gil Thomas told a reporter, "God answers prayers. People just don't know what he means to this school and these kids."

The 2004 season saw the Jackson Academy Eagles moving up to the Alabama Independent School Association's AA division from the A division. They would now play against larger schools and against tougher competition.

In the season opener, the Eagles faced Independent Methodist, a single A school. They were no match for Jackson Academy. Dillon Howard, Lee Evans, Terry Knapp, Clay Carpenter, Clay Johnston, and Zack Yeldell all scored in a 52–0 victory. The winning streak moved to sixteen.

The Eagles finally saw their streak broken against Pickens Academy, ending one that began late in the 2002 season, just a year after going winless. Another loss to Patrician Academy followed.

More losses than wins occurred over the next few weeks before Carl Madison's final game at Jackson Academy came in the 2004 season finale against Marengo Academy. It was a disappointing season by Madison's standards, but he wanted to go out a winner. First quarter touchdowns by Johnny Nichols and Dustin Taylor gave the Eagles a 14–0 lead, and they never looked back on their way to a 47–14 victory. It was Madison's 326th and final victory as a head coach in a career that spanned almost five decades.

When Madison finally announced that he would not return to coach at Jackson Academy, most were not surprised though they were disappointed.

"I felt sorry for the kids who wouldn't have him as a coach. If you play for him, you're going to love him or hate him. I ended up loving him," Travis Overstreet later said.

Paul Parham said of Madison's tenure at Jackson Academy, "There will never be anybody else to do what he did. It's just unbelievable to me what he did. . . . I honestly believe people came to watch him coach."

Rosemary Colvin, the mother of John Ryan, who quarterbacked Jackson Academy to two state championships, wasn't sure what to think of Carl Madison initially. She later became one of his biggest fans. "He had an uncanny ability to involve everybody in the community," she said.

Madison encouraged the players' mothers to organize a team meal on Thursdays and host a "Fifth Quarter" event on Friday nights after home games. "We never had a coach who took care of the details like that. . . . Madison never felt like he was too good to do some of the manual tasks," Rosemary added.

She personally witnessed Madison washing the team uniforms. She also believed Madison went beyond a football coach and cared about the whole person. Rosemary's husband Bill thought that Madison felt that a football program could have a big impact on the entire school and other sports programs at the school. He saw the effects of the success of football at Jackson Academy.

Many people witnessed the same influence at places like Ernest Ward, Milton, Forest Park, Tate, and Pine Forest. Carl Madison had an impact that went far beyond the football field.

Later when reflecting on his career, Madison stated that what he accomplished at Jackson Academy may have been his biggest thrill in coaching.

Carl Madison's final record as a high school head football coach was 326-139-7. Though there are other coaches around the country who won more games and finished with higher winning percentages, none did it quite the way he did. Multiple times he took over losing programs and turned them around quickly, not just into winners, but into powers.

In 1985, before he achieved his greatest success in the state, he was named to the Florida Athletic Coaches Association Hall of Fame. One could easily make the argument that he had three separate Hall of Fame careers in Florida: at Milton, at Tate, and at Pine Forest. What he did at each of those schools alone would justify induction. When you include his successes in Georgia and Alabama, you get an even greater understanding of his greatness. In Madison's five-state championship seasons, his teams won their playoff games by an average score of 37–10.

His greatest honor may have come in 2007 when the Florida High School Activities Association named him one of twelve coaches on the All-Century team in celebration of one hundred years of high school football in the state.

When Madison's former player Mike Killam was inducted into the Pensacola Sports Association Hall of Fame in 2015, he invited his former baseball and offensive line coach at Tate, Floyd Adams, and his head football coach, Carl Madison, to sit at his table. In his speech, he spoke about how proud he was to receive the honor and how proud he was that his two former coaches were there to celebrate with him. He spoke of their toughness and how unforgiving they were on the field but also about how much they loved the young men they coached throughout the years.

Madison and Adams both received standing ovations.

How the success of Madison teams instilled pride in the schools and communities where he coached is often mentioned, but perhaps no one sums up the impact he had better than Steve Campbell. Speaking of his experience at Tate, Campbell said, "When I think of Tate, I think of Coach Madison. The rest of it is just buildings. When I was in the ninth grade, the football team was state champion. The band was national champion. We were voted the most spirited school in the country. To me, you can attribute all of that to the influence of Coach Madison."

Madison's influence was similar almost everywhere he coached.

Madison made one final return to coaching, serving as offensive coordinator at Tate High School under former Aggie player Eddie Rigby when he was seventy-eight years old. It was a fitting place to finish a remarkable coaching career, where he had won the first of his five state championships and created Pensacola's own version of the "Big Red Machine."

For many years, the Tate team had played football at Pete Gindl Stadium. In 2021, the school chose to honor Carl Madison by naming the field at Pete Gindl Stadium after him. Games are now played on Carl Madison Field at Pete Gindl Stadium.

Madison also received the long overdue honor of being voted into the Florida High School Athletic Association Hall of Fame that same year. His legacy is established in northwest Florida and beyond as one of the great high school football coaches in the history of the game as anyone who played for him or saw him in action will attest.

POSTSCRIPT

IN MY FIRST conversation with Carl Madison's son Sky, he said, "Some people were put on the earth to do things. [My father] was put on the earth to guide all these other boys . . . and help them out and guide them through life. I used to think that he was kind of selfish and didn't want to do things with us or spend time with us, but I think he was put on this earth to give to all these other people and help them out. He knew we were okay. He made sure we were okay, but he gave to all these other people. Some of these boys didn't have anything. He genuinely cared."

Though he indeed cared deeply, more than we realized at the time, Carl Madison was tough on his players, and every one of them would attest to that. Jerry Halfacre recalled running into Jerry Pollard at a little league football game once, and they began sharing stories about Madison.

Pollard mentioned, "Those quarterbacks and kickers that played for Carl, there ain't no way in hell I'd play either one of those positions because those were the two toughest positions to play for him."

Halfacre responded, "Well, I'm the biggest idiot walking around here."

When Pollard asked why, Halfacre told him, "Because I did both,"

Scotti Madison faced the difficult situation of being both a quarterback for Coach Madison and his nephew. It seemed the coach went out of his way to demonstrate that he played no favorites. But as tough as Carl was on Scotti, Scotti's father, Charlie, told me later that he would have been even tougher.

Though Madison was tough, he never publicly blamed his players for a loss. "I'd take care of that on Monday," he later said, referring to the difficult practices that typically occurred following losses.

Madison was also tough on officials, though he believes he only had about five penalties called on him during his entire career. "And a couple of those were on purpose," he admitted.

From my own experience, I can say that one of most exciting moments of my life came as a sophomore in high school on the kickoff team for the first play of the 1981 season. Tate was the defending state champion and top-ranked team in the state of Florida. I had a moment to look around the packed stadium and take it all in. Carl Madison made that moment possible for me, and he made an untold number of those types of moments, along with even more special ones, for hundreds of young men over almost fifty years of coaching.

In January of 2021, a couple of hundred family, friends, former players, and coaches gathered in the activity hall of Hillcrest Church in Pensacola to celebrate Carl Madison's ninetieth birthday. It was an amazing time of fellowship and laughter with several speakers relating stories about the man they knew. I was fortunate to be able to speak about his history as a football player and coach over many decades. Few realized all the things he'd accomplished, and I had no idea myself until I undertook the project of writing this book. It was incredibly rewarding to me to learn more about my coach.

With the encouragement of others, I was also able to submit his name for induction to the Florida High School Athletic Association Hall of Fame in 2021. He was already a member of the Florida Athletic Coaches Hall of Fame but not the more prestigious FHSAA Hall of Fame. It was a privilege to see him selected and witness his long overdue induction in the summer of that year.

Though his approach may not have been approved by all—and he certainly ruffled many feathers over the years—he is a Hall of Famer in every sense of the word. I think I speak for most of my fellow teammates and those who played for Carl Madison elsewhere when I say I am incredibly grateful, not only for the moments I experienced playing for him but for the lessons learned.

CLINT CROCKETT
August 2021

ACKNOWLEDGEMENTS

THERE ARE SO many people who contributed to this book, some of whom don't realize how much they did by their encouragement alone. A significant part of the book comes from interviews I conducted with people close to Carl Madison including family members, former players, and fellow coaches, among others. Family members including his wife Grace, his brother Charlie, his son Sky, his daughter Becky, and his nephew Scotti all spoke with me over the years. Grace and Charlie have both passed since our interviews and are missed by everyone who knew them. Scotti was gracious enough to write the foreword for the book.

A number of other people spoke with me to answer questions and share their stories about Carl Madison over the years. They include Floyd Adams, Mike Bennett, Rodney Blunt, Paul Bowers, James Broxson, Mickey Broxson, Paul Brown, Shellie Campbell, Steve Campbell, Frank Colburn, Bill Colvin, John Ryan Colvin, Rosemary Colvin, Gene Cox, Justin Dailey, Jerry Halfacre, John Hammack, Norbert Hector Sr., Erik Hector, Karl Jernigan, Mike Killam, Keith Leonard, Jack Locklin, Travis Overstreet, Paul Parham, Jerry Pollard, Dan Shugart, Tim Thomas, and Walter Welch.

I began this book in 2006 before a lot of the material from newspapers was available online, so I spent dozens of hours doing research in libraries on microfilm and reading through old newspaper copies. I appreciate the assistance of library staff at the University of West Florida; the Atmore, Alabama public library; the Jackson, Alabama public library, and the Albany, Georgia public library.

My father, James Crockett, provided tremendous help to me. He read the manuscript numerous times and provided excellent editorial suggestions. The final version of this book would be a far lesser one without his contribution.

I have a group of friends who I played football with under Carl Madison at Tate. They include Steve Campbell, Hank Colburn, Don Halfacre, Dennis Smith, and Gordon Whatley. I am grateful for forty-plus years of friendship with them and for their encouragement with this project.

During the planning of Carl Madison's ninetieth birthday event, I worked closely with and received encouragement from Erik Hector, Dan Karp, Steve Black, Sky Madison, and Scotti Madison. I am proud to call them friends.

I am very grateful to Indigo River Publishing and the people I have worked with there, including Georgette Green, Deborah Froese, and Earl Tillinghast. They all provided outstanding suggestions to me throughout, and the resulting book is better because of their efforts.

Of course, I can't forget Carl Madison, who was gracious enough to spend a lot of time with me over the years and willing to share his thoughts on any subject I posed. When I asked about his willingness to answer some of the tougher questions, he told me that at his age, he no longer had anything to worry about.

It is a tremendous honor to say I once played for the man. It has been an incredible gift to learn more about his story and speak with so many people whose lives he influenced. He is truly one of the all-time greats. If you weren't convinced of that before, I hope that after reading his story, you now are.

SOURCES

FOREWORD

NEWSPAPERS
Pensacola News Journal (Archives University of West Florida Library)

INTERVIEWS
Carl Madison
John Ryan Colvin

CHAPTER 1: HARDSCRABBLE BEGINNINGS

NEWSPAPERS
Atmore Advance (Archives Atmore, Alabama Public Library)

WEBSITES
amarillo.com (*Amarillo Globe-News* Archives)
https://www.campgordonjohnston.com
mycarabelle.com
newspaperarchive.com (*Troy Messenger* Archives)
newspapers.com (*Atmore Advance* Archives)
newspapers.com (*Lubbock Morning Avalanche* Archives)

INTERVIEWS
Floyd Adams
Carl Madison
Charlie Madison
Walter Welch

CHAPTER 2: GETTING ESTABLISHED

NEWSPAPERS

Atlanta Constitution (Archives University of Mississippi Library)

Pensacola News (Archives University of West Florida Library)

Pensacola News Journal (Archives University of West Florida Library)

WEBSITES

northescambia.com/northwestfloridacomm.com/walnuthill

miltonfl.org/244/History

001.clayton.k12.ga.us/about/history

INTERVIEWS

Floyd Adams

Mickey Broxson

Gene Cox

Keith Leonard

Carl Madison

CHAPTER 3: ASCENDENCY

NEWSPAPERS

Atlanta Constitution (Archives University of Mississippi Library)

Atlanta Journal (Archives University of Mississippi Library)

Pensacola Journal (Archives University of West Florida Library)

Pensacola News (Archives University of West Florida Library)

Pensacola News Journal (Archives University of West Florida Library)

INTERVIEWS

Floyd Adams

Paul Bowers

Jerry Halfacre

Carl Madison

Scotti Madison

CHAPTER 4: STALLED

NEWSPAPERS

Pensacola Journal (Archives University of West Florida Library)

Pensacola News (Archives University of West Florida Library)

Pensacola News Journal (Archives University of West Florida Library))

WEBSITES

pnj.com

INTERVIEWS

Mike Bennett

Steve Campbell

Erik Hector

Norbert Hector Sr.

Keith Leonard

Carl Madison

Scotti Madison

CHAPTER 5: HEIGHTS AND DEPTHS

NEWSPAPERS

Pensacola Journal (Archives University of West Florida Library)

Pensacola News (Archives University of West Florida Library)

Pensacola News Journal (Archives University of West Florida Library)

WEBSITES

pnj.com

INTERVIEWS

Floyd Adams

Paul Brown

Shellie Campbell

Steve Campbell

Frank Colburn Sr.

Gene Cox

Erik Hector

Keith Leonard
Carl Madison
Grace Madison
Sky Madison
Tim Thomas

CHAPTER 6: TRIUMPHANT RETURN

NEWSPAPERS

Pensacola News (Archives University of West Florida Library)
Pensacola News Journal (Archives University of West Florida Library)
USA Today (Archives University of West Florida Library)

WEBSITES

pnj.com

INTERVIEWS

Mike Bennett
Rodney Blunt
John Hammack
Keith Leonard
Carl Madison
Jerry Pollard
Dan Shugart

CHAPTER 7: DECISIONS

NEWSPAPERS

Pensacola News (Archives University of West Florida Library)
Pensacola News Journal (Archives University of West Florida Library)

WEBSITES

newspaperarchive.com (Albany Herald Archives)
pnj.com

INTERVIEWS

Mike Bennett

James Broxson
Mike Killam
Carl Madison
Grace Madison
Scotti Madison
Karl Jernigan

CHAPTER 8: FINAL GLORY

NEWSPAPERS
Pensacola News Journal (Archives University of West Florida Library)

WEBSITES
pnj.com
southalabamian.com

INTERVIEWS
Steve Campbell
Bill Colvin
John Ryan Colvin
Rosemary Colvin
Justin Dailey
Mike Killam
Carl Madison
Grace Madison
Sky Madison
Paul Parham
Travis Overstreet

POSTSCRIPT

INTERVIEWS
Sky Madison
Jerry Halfacre
Carl Madison
Charlie Madison

CPSIA information can be obtained
at www.ICGtesting.com
Printed in the USA
BVHW060515110922
646602BV00009B/20